PRAISE FOR

Becoming a Better Boss

"It was an absolute pleasure to read this book. *Becoming a Better Boss* presents a practical examination of leadership. It incorporates perspectives from frontline employees, middle managers, and senior leaders to provide a comprehensive view of effective leadership. The book offers tools designed to cultivate and strengthen essential leadership competencies. Having had the privilege of working with Burl, I felt like I spent a few hours with a great friend talking about leadership and I genuinely could not put it down."

—Jason Niehaus,
President of Archbishop Moeller High School

"Burl Stamp has written one of the most honest, insightful books on management that I have read over my 40 years in leadership positions. I especially appreciated Burl's vulnerability and willingness to share lessons from his personal experience in his own leadership journey. This book is an excellent, practical guide to best management practices. I highly recommend it for new leaders as well as those who are already established – it's never too late to learn."

—William M. Behrendt,
PhD, Executive Coach and former Chief Human Resources Officer, UT Southwestern Medical Center

"In an era when disengagement and burnout dominate headlines, *Becoming a Better Boss* offers a refreshing dose of accountability. Burl Stamp reminds us that while market forces shift and generational expectations evolve, one factor remains constant: the boss matters. With humility and wisdom, Burl reframes leadership as stewardship. The best bosses support, coach, recognize, and develop the people entrusted to them. For any manager committed to building trust, strengthening engagement, and leading in a way that earns a team member's enrollment rather than compliance, this book provides both encouragement and direction."

—Leo Bottary,
author of Peernovation

"*Becoming a Better Boss* is a well-written, concise roadmap that helps leaders understand the untapped energy that can be unleashed by teaching, empowering, aligning, and mentoring the entire workforce. Burl's personal anecdotes are priceless and add immeasurable value to the book without overshadowing its core message: mentoring individuals to strengthen the team is one of the most effective ways to achieve sustained organizational success."

—Brian Smith,
former President and COO, Bon Secours Mercy Health

"*Becoming a Better Boss* is both insightful and engaging. As the workplace becomes more and more focused on AI, this book's focus on humanization and purpose is particularly timely. The second part of the book provides both practical and tactical strategies for enhancing employee engagement, as well as operating results. I would encourage anyone leading a team to use this as a resource."

— Peggy (Pepe) Finn,
Chairman & CEO, Stern Brothers & Co.

Becoming a Better Boss

Be the leader people want to follow, not just tolerate

BURL STAMP

Published by Ripples Media
Atlanta, Georgia
www.ripples.media

For more information: contact@ripples.media

First printing 2026

Cover design by Dwight Stamp
Typesetting by Najdan Mancic

ISBN 978-1-971718-14-9 (Paperback)
ISBN 978-1-971718-15-6 (Hardcover)
ISBN 978-1-971718-13-2 (eBook)
Library of Congress Control Number: 2026907498

CONTENTS

Dedicated to the memory of my friend and mentor,
Alan W. Brass, who was the best boss I've ever worked for.

FOREWORD

Whether you're the president of a large division of a Fortune 500 company or an entrepreneur starting a new venture, the quality of the people you hire to lead and support your employees on the front lines will be the most important determinant of your success.

I've done both. I spent the formative years of my career as a rising executive with May Department Stores Company before I decided to launch Build-a-Bear Workshop. When I wrote the book *The Bear Necessities of Business: Building a Company with Heart* to share what I had learned along the way, there's a reason that the first major section was titled "Being a Great Boss."

Great bosses, from the C-suite executive to the frontline supervisor, are the lifeblood of great organizations. There are moments every strong leader remembers—usually not because they felt triumphant, but because they felt *real*. It might be the first time you had to correct someone's work without crushing their confidence. Or the first time your team looked to you for a decision you didn't feel ready to make. Or the day you realized the title on your business card didn't magically confer wisdom, patience, or the ability to inspire.

If you're holding this book, you already understand something important: becoming a better boss isn't about collecting authority. It's about earning trust—again and again, in hundreds of small moments that rarely make it into performance reviews.

Aspiring bosses sometimes think leadership is demonstrated from a distance: issuing directives, monitoring results, moving people around like pieces on a chessboard. But the leaders who change us—the ones we remember years later—are rarely the ones who stood above the work. They're the ones who stepped into it. They showed up beside us. They guided without grabbing the wheel, coached without condescension, and treated progress like a shared project instead of a solo performance.

That kind of leadership isn't glamorous. It doesn't always look or feel perfect in the short term. But it's powerful—because it tells people, without a speech or slogan, **you matter, your work matters, and I'm not asking you to do anything I wouldn't do myself.**

This book is titled *Becoming a Better Boss*, and I hope you read it as an invitation to find your own personal purpose and fulfillment in leading other people. That means going well beyond the old-school command and control theory of leadership. It requires being present, curious, and willing to understand what your people actually face on an ordinary Tuesday. Because here's what happens when leaders step out from behind the desk and into the workflow: you learn faster what's broken, what's brilliant, and what your team needs to win.

Just as importantly, your team learns something about you. When they see you doing real work, asking questions, and admitting what you don't know, you become more approachable. You become a person, not a position. That shift alone can unlock honesty, creativity, and the kind of problem-solving that no strategy deck can produce.

You'll notice as you move through these chapters that "better boss" doesn't mean "tougher leader." It doesn't mean louder, sharper, or more intimidating. In fact, the era of fear-based leadership is fading for good reasons: people don't bring their best to places where they feel small. Real leadership is rooted in respect—the kind that's shown in how you correct mistakes, how you deliver criticism, and whether you listen with the intent to understand rather than the intent to control.

Respect also changes what you do with mistakes. At a very young age I learned the value of stepping up, being courageous, and making mistakes from my first-grade teacher Mrs. Grace. Every week, she gave the Red Pencil Award, not to the student who was perfect, but rather to the one who made the most mistakes. She wisely recognized that mistakes simply presented more opportunities to learn.

Some companies say they value innovation, then punish every misstep like it was sabotage. But if you want initiative, you have to make room for learning. You have to reward smart risk-taking and help people distinguish between "I tried something" and "I repeated the same error twice." When you treat mistakes as opportunities to learn and improve, your team stops hiding problems and starts solving them.

You'll also find something else here that might surprise you: becoming a better boss can—and should—include joy. Not performative "fun," not distractions masquerading as culture, but the kind of environment where people can breathe, laugh, celebrate milestones, and feel like work is a place they belong rather than a place they endure. Done well, this isn't fluff; it's fuel. It builds energy, loyalty, and momentum—without sacrificing standards or results.

Of course, results do matter. A good boss keeps score, not just of revenue and output, but of the experience people create for customers and for each other. The best leaders don't hoard praise; they circulate it. They build systems that reinforce what "good" looks like, and they make recognition specific and visible.

Perhaps the most powerful benefit of this approach to leadership is the understanding—and insistence—that ideas don't have to travel uphill through layers of permission. Your frontline people are not just labor; they are insight. They see friction before you do. They hear customer truths in real time. When you make yourself accessible in a genuine, transparent, consistent way, you gain a direct line to improvement that competitors can't copy.

If you're ready to become a better boss, you don't need to completely reshape who you are by following a strict checklist of ideal leadership qualities. In fact, trying to become someone you are not is one of the best ways to become a rigid, unapproachable, disconnected leader. Rather, you just need to embrace a few enduring behaviors: show up, pitch in, listen intently, coach thoughtfully, respect relentlessly, and create conditions where people can do meaningful work with pride.

That's what this book is about.

So, turn the page—not as an assessment on how you've led so far, but as a personal commitment to continually becoming a better boss for the people who are counting on you every day.

Maxine Clark

Founder, Build-a-Bear Workshop® and Delmar DevINe
Author, The Bear Necessities of Business: Building a Company with Heart

INTRODUCTION

No one is ever really ready to become a boss.

Think about how we all become bosses for the first time. You've been a star individual performer who's separated yourself from the rest of the pack by working hard, taking on tough projects, and delivering great results. Your boss recognizes and appreciates what you bring to the company, so you're rewarded with a promotion to manager. What they don't tell you is that the skills, behaviors, and mindset that will make you successful as a leader of other people are very different from those that made you stand out as an individual member of the team.

But the problem of making the transition from worker bee to boss goes beyond adequate preparation. In some ways, the characteristics that made you a company wunderkind are ones that can make you a terrible boss. Up until now, it's largely been all about you. You're competitive, goal-oriented, and willing to do whatever it takes to set yourself apart from the crowd. At heart, you believe that you can do things better than anyone else in your department. Sure, you get along well with your colleagues. But even your commitment to teamwork is framed in your mind as a character trait you need to develop to succeed individually.

This book is about the transition from successful employee to successful boss. The journey is one with many twists and turns that includes both breakthroughs and setbacks, but it starts with one self-reflective question that all great people-centric leaders continue to ask themselves throughout their careers.

Am I a good boss?

That's a question that not nearly enough of us who have fellow human beings working for us ask ourselves often enough. But given the new realities of today's labor force, it's become one of the most important questions smart leaders contemplate related to their own professional development, work satisfaction, and personal impact on organizational success.

Outside of family and close friends, nothing has a bigger impact on our overall happiness, outlook on life, and sense of self-worth than our work. Our work either fascinates and fulfills or drains and discourages us. Our experience at work influences our relationships with others and our sense of well-being, even when we're off-the-clock.

So, what most influences the way employees feel about their jobs? According to a 2017 Gallup report, 70 percent of the variance in employee engagement can be explained by one thing: the person an employee reports to.[1] No other component of the workplace environment–compensation, innovative benefits, environmental factors, or peer relationships–comes anywhere close. Simply, if you have a great boss, you're more engaged, fulfilled, and happy. If you work for a bad boss, your disposition and overall outlook on life–both personally and professionally–take a hit.

Research studies that quantify the impact bosses have on their employees are important. The personal experience individuals have working for other people is even more powerful. In my work with managers and their employees, I've tried to become a more observant, astute student of their experience over the past decade. Watching closely to really understand the emotional impact a boss has on employees' well-being provided the inspiration for this book. It has been humbling and heartening to witness the incredible effect a great boss can have on the development, success, and well-being of staff. It is just as disheartening to watch how a mediocre boss can suck the very life out of a team.

During my career, I've tried to dial up my own self-reflection and sensitivity to the kind of boss I've become. In many ways, this book is my own leadership memoir, documenting my personal journey to becoming a stronger, more people-centric leader. My elevated sense of self-awareness and personal development certainly didn't happen overnight. But there were major ah-hah moments along the way that accelerated my resolve to become a better boss.

One of the most powerful of these moments came while I was a member of the executive team at St. Louis Children's Hospital early in my career. Because I worked hard and had some lucky breaks along the way, I became a vice president at Children's before I turned 30. That arbitrary but personally meaningful achievement lulled me into the false sense of assurance that I must be a great boss. A group exercise during a leadership retreat helped burst that bubble of exaggerated confidence — even arrogance — that I was living in.

While I've always appreciated the advantages of strong teamwork, I've never been a fan of traditional "team-building" exercises. Thankfully, no one has ever asked me to fall backwards off a table into the arms of waiting colleagues. The team-building exercise during this retreat was far less risky and far more enlightening. It helped me begin to recognize and understand some of my leadership blind spots and developmental opportunities as a boss. The retreat facilitator made us break into two large groups, put on blindfolds, and hold hands in long lines in the middle of an open field. His colleague was at the far end of the pasture with a cow bell. Our goal was to move toward the sound of the cow bell as a group. The goal seemed straightforward: the group that found and touched the guy with the cow bell first, wins.

This seemingly simple exercise was a lot more challenging and frustrating than it sounded on the surface. The linked line of my colleagues was long and incredibly tough to collectively steer. The guy with the cow bell was constantly moving — and likely taking great pleasure in watching us struggle. I was stuck in the middle of the line, with little ability to influence what was happening at either end. At one point, I heard the cow bell close to me, so I told the person whose hand I was holding that I was going to break the chain, grab the cow bell guy, and then come back to retrieve the rest of our team. I was feeling really proud of the fact that we "won," until the group debrief about how the exercise made everyone feel. Someone in our chain spoke up.

"They just left us behind, and we had no idea where we were supposed to go. I felt kind of abandoned."

Ouch. It was like a self-awareness bomb exploded at my feet that was enlightening and totally ego-deflating at the same time.

I often did leave others behind. Winning was incredibly important to me. And I defined myself by my personal achievements.

That experience and the subsequent advice of a trusted colleague made me start to appreciate what being a great boss was really all about. I needed to become far less consumed with individual success and far more focused on how I could help members of my team be most successful.

A year or two after that retreat, I was named president and CEO of Phoenix Children's Hospital. As I left my team at St. Louis Children's, I asked each individual who reported to me to give me some advice: what should I continue to work on to be a better leader in my new job? The most insightful, candid advice came from my long-time friend and colleague Nancy Litzinger. Nancy shared, "You run really fast. If you can slow down a little bit every so often to let your team catch up, they'll love you for it." It's advice that I've never forgotten.

A leader? Or a boss?

When managers think about their role in an organization, I often hear, "Oh, I don't want to be a boss; I want to be a leader." I've heard that bias voiced many times and expressed the same aspiration in the same way early in my career. The sentiment is understandable, but it's also disconnected from the day-to-day realities of what it means to be a better, competent leader of *people*, not just strategies and ideas.

Unfortunately, part of the reason we aspire to be called a leader rather than a boss is the underlying perception each term carries in society. People think of leaders as visionary, innovative, inspirational, and trailblazing. We often associate a different set of adjectives with bosses: demeaning, capricious, and domineering. As a result, the term leader just sounds a lot sexier and appealing than the term boss.

But regardless of what we aspire to be or how we hope to be viewed, the reality is that the colloquial term we all use to describe the person we work for is "boss."

Whatever we call them, frontline leaders carry a tremendous degree of responsibility. But too often, these responsibilities are only viewed through the lens of traditional business metrics:

growth, expense management, customer satisfaction/loyalty, quality, and profitability. After all, the "hard numbers" define success and drive shareholder value, right?

But there's another set of metrics standing directly between leaders and achievement of those KPIs: employee engagement, turnover, and productivity. It's tough to make progress on the bottom line when you are mired in vacancies and burnout.

In a post-pandemic economy, companies increasingly are sounding the alarm around workforce metrics and culture. Never before has the link between full employee engagement and the achievement of traditional hard-number success metrics been more direct — and so vexing.

In her article "Eight Essential Qualities of Successful Leaders,"[2] Harvard Business School professor Linda Hill explains that her research reveals the following characteristics necessary for successful leadership:

- ▶ Authenticity
- ▶ Curiosity
- ▶ Analytical prowess
- ▶ Adaptability
- ▶ Creativity
- ▶ Comfort with ambiguity
- ▶ Resilience
- ▶ Empathy

What strikes me about her list is there are basically two groups of leadership skills. One emphasizes our interactions and leadership of people (authenticity, creativity, resilience, and empathy). The other group focuses on our deftness in analysis and leading strategic initiatives (curiosity, analytical prowess, adaptability, and comfort with ambiguity). Just because you think strategically and are adept at charting new paths for growth doesn't mean you are a great leader of people, or in more common vernacular, a good boss. In today's challenging and evolving employment market, strong bosses who are talented people-centric leaders offer a major competitive advantage for organizations.

Of course, situational factors also impact how important strategy-centric vs. people-centric aspects of leadership are. Leaders closer to the top of the organization by design and responsibility have to be focused on longer-term, more strategic issues that are going to spur growth, enhance market position, and/or improve financial results. Frontline leaders impact the success of the organization in different ways. They take responsibility for making sure that brilliant strategies and programs are effectively implemented. And success in implementation is determined largely by how engaged, committed, and well-prepared staff are in the trenches. In other words, being a great boss to work for is especially critical in middle management so that organizational strategies crafted at 30,000 feet actually work when they hit the ground.

The two introspective questions leaders should ask themselves

Even if frontline leaders are not actively contemplating the question of whether or not they are a good boss, we can be sure that their employees are asking themselves a related question every day: *Do I have a good boss whom I want to continue working for?* Recognizing this reality and using it as a springboard to more thoughtful, purposeful personal development is something that great people-centric leaders come to early in their careers.

Great leaders recognize early that leadership development is not a straight nor smooth path. Like any effective organizational improvement strategy, personal improvement is a journey. The best bosses are always looking for ways to get better, especially with the organizational recovery challenges that the pandemic and subsequent workforce shortages have thrown at them.

One's introspective path in leadership development happens in many ways, but I've found that one question is often a great place to start:

> *Who's the best person I've ever worked for, and what did they do differently that I want to emulate?*

Reading books or attending workshops on leadership theory can be helpful in understanding best practices. But there's nothing quite like seeing a great leader in action.

How did she make you feel? What specific practices encouraged you to work harder to succeed — both personally and professionally? What did he do that made you want to stay and grow with the organization? What specific behaviors set this leader apart and would cause you to want to work for them again?

The more specific you can be in reflecting on what this leader did well every day, the more helpful this introspective exercise will be. Focusing not just on the *what* but also on the *how* and *why* is most enlightening and helps isolate the philosophies and behaviors that truly distinguish outstanding leaders.

So, start with the recognition that she was a great communicator, for example. Then, think about why that came to mind.

How did she listen? How did she clearly explain complex ideas and put different issues into context? What vehicles and venues did she use to make communication consistent across the team?

Close behind thinking about the best person you've ever worked for is a question that looks at the other end of the spectrum:

> *Who is the worst boss I've ever worked for, and what did they do that I want to avoid inflicting on my own team?*

Introspectively looking back on your own experience with an ineffective boss is often illuminating in a different way than just looking at the positive aspects of great leaders. In our work with leadership teams across diverse organizations, when we ask managers to reflect on this question, we find their responses are immediate, guttural, and usually far more emotional than their reflections on the great bosses they've worked for. Like in most aspects of life, our negative experiences can be far more jarring, painfully memorable, and formative than positive ones.

Research proves that humans are hardwired with a negativity bias, an evolutionary trait that prioritizes negative information as a survival mechanism. In our work life, this bias means negative events often have a greater psychological impact than equally intense positive ones.

So how might research on the exaggerated impact of negative experiences help us better understand current disturbing trends in employee turnover, disengagement, and burnout? Simply, negative experiences working for a bad boss can have an inordinately significant impact on the way we feel about work and, as a result, how loyal we'll be to a company. Research has shown that for multiple reasons, today's employees actually expect their tenure in a new job to be shorter than in the past. If they end up working for a non-supportive boss, that only accelerates their departure. Clearly, companies have to work harder today than in the past to earn employees' loyalty. What they get day-to-day from the person they work for is the most influential factor in their engagement and commitment longer-term.

"But this next generation of employees have completely unrealistic expectations," I often hear from frustrated managers. And that may well be true given the social, economic, and political environment that they've grown up in. But age and experience doesn't make us immune to poor leadership. Personal well-being and commitment to their company are diminished by a mediocre boss just as much for GenXers and Boomers and for their younger colleagues. My personal experience has proven to me that's true.

With decades of work experience behind me, I've seen it all, both as a boss and as a subordinate. I pride myself on being able to deal with whatever is thrown my way and letting things roll off my back. But a recent experience has convinced me that I'm just as vulnerable to the burden of a lousy boss as I've ever been.

Since I started my firm over 20 years ago, many people have commented on how great it must be to be your own boss. But I have lots of bosses; they're called clients. The good news is that the vast majority of people I work for are gifted, supportive leaders in phenomenal companies. I learn important things from them every day, and much of that knowledge is reflected in the pages of this book.

But occasionally, I encounter a leadership lemon. That happened recently in an amazing organization where I've completed countless projects over many years. I respected all the executives in the division where I was working, and I was proud of the progress we were making together on strengthening leadership practices and outcome. Then a new executive from outside the organization joined the team.

Despite the fact that I reached out to him immediately to share our work and get his input, I felt a distinct chill in even my first meeting. By our third meeting, he was demanding that I stop talking to other leaders on the team without his knowledge and approval. "How much is this costing and what budget is it coming out of?" he angrily asked.

As I walked out of his office that day, my enthusiasm for the entire project and all that we had accomplished evaporated. Thankfully, we were near the end of the engagement with only a few items left to complete. My team and I, of course, delivered exactly what we had promised. But the work was painful. Tasks that should have taken hours required days. Simply, my heart just wasn't in it anymore. While I knew I would miss all of the wonderful people we'd had the privilege to work with along the way, as we wrapped up during our final week, I was unexpectedly happy to get the hell out of there.

About this book

Most executives admit that their middle managers have the toughest jobs in their organizations. During the pandemic, those jobs only got tougher. The lingering effects of that defining period for management will likely be felt for years to come by individuals and the companies they work for.

The first half of this book explores how we got to where we are in terms of leadership theory and practice over the past several decades. There are reasons why bad bosses are too prevalent and improving workplace culture requires first a shift in thinking about what defines a great boss in today's challenging labor environment.

The second half of the book gets more tactical. What are the specific, day-to-day leadership skills and practices that make someone a terrific person to work for? We emphasize not only the "what" but also the "how" and "why" associated with best people-centric leadership practices since the way these practices are viewed and adopted significantly impacts how they are received by our teams.

As employees, we've all spent time in a real-life "leadership lab" in the workplace. That should help us as a leader reflect on what works and what doesn't as a boss. Ultimately, helping you answer the question, "Am I the kind of boss that I'd want to work for?" is what this book is all about.

PART
ONE

Why Are There So Many Bad Bosses?

I f you've never had a bad boss, you're in the minority. A Monster global poll in 2014 asked 2,555 employees to rate their boss on a scale from 1 to 5.[3] Half of respondents rated their boss a "1" or "2," with nearly one-third saying the person they worked for was "horrible." Only 15 percent rated their boss as "excellent."

If research is so clear and compelling regarding the influence a manager has on their team, why are there so many bad bosses? Specific reasons vary from company to company and even from team to team within the same organization. But a foundational reason many *companies* have tolerated bad bosses is that their *employees* have tolerated bad bosses. Limited or no mandate to significantly improve the quality of frontline leadership has roots in both structural and cultural issues.

Structurally, companies over the past century adopted compensation and benefits strategies that encouraged employees to stay in spite of suboptimal working conditions. The dramatic, durable impact of the Great Depression in the 1930s meant that most individuals considered themselves lucky to have any regular income, even when they may have felt ignored, discounted, or even abused by their bosses. This fear-based loyalty was further solidified in the mid-1940s with the advent of two major additions to traditional compensation: employer-sponsored health insurance and defined benefit pension/retirement plans. The reasons these strategies were originally embraced and how they've changed over the past decade says much about where we've been—and where we might be going—related to employee engagement. Interestingly, both of these employee benefit innovations grew not out of companies' desire to support the well-being of their workforce but rather to indirectly boost total compensation and better compete for limited talent.

As America entered World War II, there was growing, well-justified concern that rampant inflation would threaten the military effort and undermine the domestic economy. In response to these concerns, President Roosevelt championed, and Congress passed, the 1942 Stabilization Act, which severely limited employers' ability to raise wages. That's when companies became convinced that providing health insurance and guaranteed retirement/pension plans were the only effective ways to attract workers from competing firms.

While health insurance and pensions were initially focused on recruitment, they also ended up being an effective retention strategy. During the Depression, Americans watched as millions were plunged into poverty, especially the elderly. Even optimistic, resourceful workers who adamantly believed they could find some kind of work regardless of economic conditions were terrified by the possibility of being financially wiped out by an unexpected, catastrophic expense like a major illness or injury. Beyond immediate worries, many were concerned about what their senior years might look like when they couldn't work. Any employee contemplating the idea of leaving a company, even if it was for a better job and potentially a better boss, had to factor in the risks of walking away from their current employer's health and pension plans. Remember that before the Affordable Care Act was enacted in 2014, restrictions on pre-existing conditions and longer eligibility waiting periods were common.[4] And pensions were usually structured to favor longer-term employees, who would hit higher retirement payment tiers with increasing years of service.

Today, many of those loyalty-focused mechanisms have been minimized or completely abandoned, both by employers themselves or by changing government programs or regulations. Most companies have moved to defined contribution retirement plans, which allow employees to take their retirement money with them. (There is often a vesting issue to consider in the early years of employment.) The value of company-sponsored health insurance has decreased for many workers, as shared premium payments along with higher deductibles and co-payments rise. With these changes, the structural and psychological barriers to leaving a job have diminished substantially.

Beyond structural issues related to compensation, benefits, and security, there are numerous factors related to organizational culture that either ignore or actually perpetuate the problem of bad bosses.

Strong people skills often are not what get you promoted

The leap from star individual performer to supervisor of other people is one of the most difficult transitions most of us make during our careers. Our responsibilities, the nature of our day-to-day work, and how the organization measures our performance change dramatically. What made this passage even more challenging for me was the fact that no one warned me of just how jarring it would be. The company wants you to be successful in your new role, but not all of the people who are now working for you may share that same feeling.

Given the skills and behaviors that made us successful early in our career, most new managers understandably fall back on and try to replicate past accomplishments when the going starts getting rough. If there's a problem, we try to fix it alone because that's what star individual performers do. We also believe, at least to some degree, that we're the smartest person in the room and best equipped to solve issues; after all, we just got promoted over all our peers. Fixing problems should be our sole responsibility now that we're in charge.

But as a leader, that approach is less likely to be successful, and it puts more burden on our shoulders than we should realistically carry alone. An example from my work with a new manager illustrates why.

As is usually the case, this new department manager had been rewarded with a promotion and supervisory responsibility after performing exceptionally well in her staff role. For one of her first staff meetings, she came prepared with a detailed agenda, beautiful PowerPoint presentation, informative handouts ... and a sense that everything in the meeting would go exactly as she had planned. Then one of her more experienced team members spoke up in response to a quality report she had presented.

"You know, this process never has worked right, and I'm not surprised our metrics are always below target," she declared. "I think the problem is in how we're prioritizing these steps, which is frustrating both us and our customers. What do you guys think about starting with different information, which might help us avoid these wasted steps in the process?" she asked her new manager and the team as a whole.

As an observer sitting in the back row of the room, I was thrilled by where it looked like this conversation was going. My experience is that frontline staff are often great at identifying the problem, but not so good at contributing to solutions. This insightful staff member contributed both.

Then I watched the response of the new manager. While, to her credit, she didn't immediately object to the employee's observation and suggestions, she also didn't encourage the shared problem-solving opportunity the discussion presented. Her nonverbal reaction showed she was clearly upset by the conversation, and she found a way to quickly move on to the next meticulously planned agenda item.

As the meeting broke up, I asked the manager to stick around for a few minutes so that we could debrief. I asked how she thought the meeting went overall.

"Well, we got through all of the information that I needed to share with them, so I think it went well," she replied. "But there were also a few rough spots. I need to do a better job of anticipating those and not let the conversation go off course like that again."

I used this opening to ask her about the idea her employee suggested to address the lagging quality metric.

"You seemed very uncomfortable with the points your team member made regarding the process that isn't working. Tell me about what you were thinking and what upset you about that conversation," I asked.

Then the emotional flood gates opened.

"Didn't you hear what she said?" she asked in frustration. "That criticism was pointed directly at me. I'm the boss now, and I'm responsible for making sure that things go well and that problems are fixed. I didn't appreciate her criticism of me in front of the whole group," she continued, her emotional tone escalating as she shared how the experience made her feel.

"Whoa, whoa, whoa," I insisted. "I think you're being too hard on yourself and taking on more than your share of responsibility in this situation. Yes, you're the boss now. But that doesn't mean you have to personally take on responsibility for identifying and fixing every problem by yourself."

We went on to talk about all the positive aspects of that interaction during the staff meeting and why encouraging frontline staff to be involved in problem-solving usually results in better solutions with stronger buy-in from the team. I emphasized that in high-performing teams, we want people to respectfully speak up — which the staff member did in this situation — so that communication remains open and transparent across the team. While she listened carefully, her non-verbals were telling me that these were all foreign concepts, and she wasn't sure she was fully buying into my philosophy, which sounded way too idealistic and unrealistic to her.

Beyond the immediate, unproductive frustration this new manager was feeling with her team, there was a much bigger, long-term dilemma she was setting up for herself. If she didn't believe her staff should be involved in problem-solving, they wouldn't either. In this kind of work environment, staff start believing that when things go wrong it is their manager's fault; they have no shared responsibility for recognizing the problem and contributing their best ideas to fix it. As leaders, when we don't invite our staff to contribute to improvement, we're indirectly sending the message that we're not interested in their ideas or experiences — and that we think we're much smarter than they are.

Bad bosses are usually good people protected by their peers and superiors

When you ask people to describe a bad boss, you are likely to hear adjectives like mean, ruthless, uncaring, arrogant, and power-hungry. From popular culture, people think of Mr. Burns from *The Simpsons*, Miranda Priestly from *The Devil Wears Prada*, or Frank Hart from the film *Nine to Five*.

In reality, most bad bosses are not bad people. They don't want bad things to happen to their employees; they do want their team to succeed and are trying to achieve the goals that the company has set for them. But they often do and say things that don't encourage teamwork, hold people appropriately accountable, or recognize strong contributions. Quite unlike cruel tyrants like Burns, Priestly, and Hart, most bad bosses share more characteristics with Michael Scott from *The Office*. Michael is oblivious to how his comments and actions affect his team, but at the end of the day, his employees know that he means well. Like many bad bosses, Michael's problem is not that he doesn't care about his employees. His challenge and blind spot are that he cares too much about being everyone's best friend and being liked. His insecurity in many ways is at the core of his weak leadership.

It is natural to feel empathy for a bad boss who is a good person. Remember that one of the key characteristics that Dr. Linda Hill included on her list of eight essential qualities of leaders is empathy. Senior leaders know what their middle managers are up against and sympathize with the pressure they are under. Unfortunately, senior leaders' empathy for the plight of the middle manager often causes them to look past the impact poor leadership skills and practices are having on the people who work for them. In strong, healthy, results-oriented company cultures, senior leaders seek to understand and empathize with the plight of frontline staff, too.

So, if bad bosses are usually good people, shouldn't we be able to reduce or eliminate the problems they create for frontline staff? Conceptually, yes. But the next reason I believe there are so many bad bosses prevents that.

Companies under-invest in developing and supporting their frontline leaders

During my career as a healthcare executive and then adviser to other executives, I've had the opportunity to work with and learn from many accomplished, visionary leaders. In many conversations with them over the years, I've often asked, "Do you believe you invest enough in the development of your middle managers?" I've never had anyone answer with an unqualified, resounding, "Yes."

More support and professional development to help frontline leaders be better bosses is a well-recognized need that has been ignored for budgetary, logistic, or philosophical reasons for a long time. But with rising turnover and burnout, coupled with mounting pressures to make progress on financial, quality, and operational issues, organizations have more reason than ever to help their hard-working, dedicated frontline leaders be successful.

Something else has changed, too. It's not just organizations that are recognizing the need for better middle management support. Today, it's the frontline leaders themselves boldly speaking up and admitting they need help. Poorly prepared and inadequately supported frontline leaders create a long-term organizational problem that goes beyond the immediate impact their struggles have on their teams. Frustration and burnout among their ranks is causing *their* turnover to increase. I often hear staff members sympathize with the challenges they clearly see managers are up against and openly concede, "You couldn't pay me enough to take that job." Increasing challenges facing middle managers are not just an immediate problem. The likely candidates for the next generation of frontline managers are questioning whether the job is one where they can be happy — and successful.

Whether frontline leaders have adequate professional development goes beyond the question of how much training is available. The more important question may be related to content and direction: is the training we're providing helping them develop the right skills? And then, are we helping them adopt, consistently implement, and sustain people-centric best leadership practices?

Over the past 20 years, corporate "universities" have become increasingly popular in many companies. Designed to support leadership development, these programs produce high-quality educational content, often in collaboration with local colleges and universities. Organizations feel good about offering these types of programs, and leaders appreciate the opportunity to participate.

But given the new realities of the labor market and dramatic shifts in how the next generation of employees feel about work, are these types of programs enough to reverse trends in turnover and staff engagement? Are these programs designed to make managers feel good about the opportunity to attend a workshop or to meaningfully change their behaviors in a sustainable way so that they will be better, more successful bosses?

In medicine, some therapies and drugs may reassure a patient that something is being done without actually helping them get better. For example, in a 2017 article in the peer-reviewed journal *The BMJ,* authors reported: "Most new oncology drugs authorized by the EMA (European Medicines Agency) in 2009-2013 came onto the market without clear evidence that they improved the quality or quantity of patients' lives."[5]

Does the same emphasis on "inputs" vs. "outcomes" happen in leadership training?

Middle managers appreciate theoretical leadership topics that take a more *academic approach* (teaching the mind to think), but today many are asking for specific, tactical training that follows a more *behavioral approach* (teaching new skills and practices). And the skills and practices they need most are the ones that will help them reengage frontline staff, reduce turnover, and improve operating results.

To ensure success and maximize return-on-investment from leadership development, organizations should embrace the same disciplined thinking that underpins operational improvement strategies: it's the *results,* not the *input,* that matter.

Organizational culture often perpetuates the problem of bad bosses

Early in my career, I had the good fortune of working for many great bosses who taught me much about strong, people-centric leadership. Their wisdom is woven into virtually every page of this book.

I've also had the misfortune of working for a few bad bosses. I learned a lot from them, too, and in many ways their lessons are just as powerful and influential as those I took away from my experiences working for terrific leaders. One experience in particular gave me great insight into why there are so many more bad bosses than there should be in American businesses.

"I will never compliment you, so don't expect to get any positive feedback from me," an early boss told me one day as we were wrapping up a meeting in her office. "If you are doing things really well, that just means you're doing your job."

Her final comment to me as I was anxious to walk out of her office was by far the most revealing and gave me great insight into what I viewed as a warped leadership philosophy. "I'm only going to criticize you when you've done something wrong *because that's the way my boss raised me.*"

As I walked out of her office, I remember my immediate reaction like it was yesterday: I've got to get out of here.

"They watch our walk much more than they listen to our talk," is a phrase I use often in leadership workshops to emphasize the importance of modeling the best practices we hope to see adopted by our staff. The same holds true in passing down flawed leadership philosophy and practices from generation to generation of managers.

But the most important thing I learned from working for the boss I described above is that there is never a single leadership culture in any organization larger than a handful of people. I worked for several bosses during my time with the company I described above, and I characterize one of them as one of the strongest leaders I've ever met. How can variability in leadership practices be that pronounced in the same company?

There's a reason that Gallup research has revealed that 70 percent of the variance in employee engagement is explained by the boss an employee reports to. Individuals view what's commonly referred to as "organizational culture" through their experiences in their immediate work team, not the company overall. The people whom a manager has worked for, in other words their bosses, have enormous impact on their developing leadership philosophy and practices. In many ways, it's akin to the dynamics of fraternity hazing; what was good for me as a pledge is going to be good for you, as well.

To reduce the number of bad bosses and impact staff engagement and workplace culture at scale, companies must become adept at identifying the gaps in people-centric leadership that don't align with their values and vision for the kind of employment organization they desire to be. The leadership philosophy and practices that each manager follows can't simply be left to chance and influenced primarily by the bad bosses they may have worked for during their formative years.

CHAPTER 2

The Better
Boss Mindset

D ecades of research on what makes the work environment most appealing and productive provides us with comprehensive lists of tactical, evidence-based practices that improve staff engagement, retention, and personal fulfillment. These lists can indeed help leaders prioritize practices that are going to make a difference in team members' experience, commitment, loyalty, and individual success. In fact, you're going to find my version of these research-based practices in the back third of this book.

But checklists alone are not the answer.

Even the best, research-based list of proven leadership practices will fail if the tasks are perfunctorily implemented with a checklist mentality. The best bosses understand that checklists provide only a foundational framework; their ability to successfully lead, mentor, and support people is more dependent on how they *think* about their role as a leader than on routinely checking off leadership tasks.

So, what's wrong with leadership checklists? Nothing, if they are used in the right way and for the right reasons.

In 2009, celebrated author, speaker, and public health researcher Dr. Atul Gawande released the book *The Checklist Manifesto*.[6] Widely hailed among healthcare leaders as an essential read for professionals committed to improving patient safety and quality, the book provided breakthrough but practical advice on standardizing elements of daily personal as well as professional life.

Ironically, the inspiration for *The Checklist Manifesto* was emotional, not simply practical. Dr. Gawande explained that he wrote the book after hearing the story of a young child who survived a fall into a frozen pond. He learned the physician who saved the child's life relied heavily on checklists. The moving story is a great example of using checklists for the right reasons, in the right situations, and in the right way. The powerful, life-changing results speak for themselves.

The danger in relying on any single management concept or checklist too heavily is that it is seldom applicable nor effective in all situations.

A screwdriver is a fine tool, but not when you encounter a nail.

Relying too much on checklists when dealing with human beings and how to best engage and support them can backfire, even for well-intentioned, dedicated bosses.

A story shared by a good friend many years ago provides a strong lesson for how a checklist mentality can go wrong. His daughter had recently graduated with her degree in nursing and joined a major, well-respected hospital. As she got her feet on the ground, she was living with her parents to save some money.

In the mail one day my friend found a hand-addressed envelope for his daughter. The return address was the hospital where she worked, including her manager's name. When his daughter got home, he immediately handed her the envelope and asked, "What do you think this is from the hospital?"

Opening the envelope revealed a notecard with the hospital logo printed on the front and a short, hand-written note inside. The generic message thanked her for joining the hospital and being a great team member.

"Wow, that's great dear," my friend beamed. "I'm so proud of you."

His daughter's reaction was not what he expected. Rolling her eyes, she shrugged and said matter-of-factly, "She met her quota this month," as she tossed the card in the trash.

It was well-known among the staff that bosses were required to write ten thank you notes to employees each month. In other words, hand-written thank you notes came from a checklist, not a place of authentic appreciation.

Great bosses develop a different mindset than checklist managers. Their actions come from a place of genuine interest in the employees who report to them, not simply checking boxes and achieving their monthly financial and operating metrics.

The characteristics of a people-centric mindset, of course, vary as much as do the characteristics of a great boss. But here are seven foundational philosophies that define the best leaders of people.

1.   Mentoring my team is my most important job.

Coming to this realization is one of the most important break-throughs individual star performers have to make in their transition to becoming a better boss. From a practical stand-point, new leaders have to accept and internalize the fact that the determinants of their individual success have shifted from the things that *they* do well to the things that *others* do well. Helping others be at their best becomes the primary motivator of great bosses.

This shift in mindset to helping others be at their best sounds terribly altruistic on the surface, but the reality is that there's a selfish aspect to thinking differently about your role: the success of your team becomes a primary determinant of your personal success. When your department does well, your stock rises in the eyes of your bosses. When your team struggles, it can completely derail your career.

I learned this the hard way in my first supervisory role. Among the employees I inherited, one individual had been a challenge for years. He was strong-willed, fiercely independent, and prided himself on being somewhat of a rebel. When we were peers, we got along great. In fact, he could be incredibly funny, and I enjoyed getting together with him and other colleagues after work.

Then I became his boss.

While the early days seemed fine, it became increasingly clear that he was not happy about reporting to a youngster (I was probably almost half his age) instead of the more seasoned director he had previously worked for. We were both testing limits, but I was becoming increasingly frustrated because his responses to my suggestions and direction felt patronizing and dismissive. That frustration boiled over during a particularly hectic, stressful day when he pushed back at the wrong time. Uncharacteristically, I blew up. His strong-willed side kicked in, and he aggressively blew up right back at me. Word of the ugly encounter spread through the rest of the team quickly.

Calmer heads prevailed, and I thought I had successfully recovered. But a few weeks later during the annual performance appraisal discussion with my boss, the primary theme completely shifted from my personal accomplishments to the fact that I was not managing this employee well. His parting words stung: "You're not a very strong leader."

My emotions walking out of his office that day ran the gamut from disbelief to anger to self-doubt. Whether my boss's assessment of my early leadership potential was right or wrong, he helped me begin to understand that the rest of my career trajectory largely would be determined by the performance of those who reported to me, not just what I accomplished.

2.   We're lucky talented people choose to work here.

How often have you heard an old-school boss say (or at least think), "Hey, they should consider themselves lucky to have a job."

This mindset probably traces some of its roots all the way back to the Great Depression, when individuals did indeed feel lucky to have any job at all. I still remember time as a kid with my grandparents, who spent a good part of their early working life during the Depression. That frightening, discouraging time influenced the way they thought about life and work until they died many decades later. It instilled in them the belief that steady work was the best work ... and that you always cleaned your plate so as not to waste precious food that someone had produced, prepared, and paid for.

While my grandfather was always exceptionally supportive of me, I'll never forget what seemed at the time an uncharacteristic reaction to my decision to go back to graduate school. I had landed my first job a few years earlier at Research Medical Center in Kansas City in the middle of a severe recession. The unemployment rate when I graduated from college was over 10 percent.

While he didn't tell me outright that I was making a bad decision, he came close. "It sure seems like you're giving up a great job there at the hospital," he remarked, overlooking the great upside benefits that I believed overshadowed the short-term risk.

Individuals like my grandfather had become the first generation of bosses after the Great Depression and carried with them the lessons — and the scars — of living through a time when almost 1 out of 4 Americans were out of work. They felt lucky to have a job. And the people who worked for them should feel lucky, too.

So, what changed? When did many employees stop feeling lucky just to have a job?

Certainly, employee attitudes toward work didn't change overnight nor for a single reason. But a significant pivot in corporate culture that took hold in the 1970s is, I believe, at the heart of the shift in employees' underlying attitudes about work.

In a 2013 Washington Post article titled "Maximizing shareholder value: the goal that changed corporate America," author Jia Lynn Yang lays out the case for how a major change in business strategy, culture and mindset played a role in how employees think about their employers. Yang writes:

"It used to be a given that the interests of corporations and communities ... were closely aligned. But no more. Across the United States, as companies continue posting record profits, workers face high unemployment and stagnant wages.

"Driving this change is a deep-seated belief that took hold in corporate America a few decades ago and has come to define today's economy — that a company's primary purpose is to maximize shareholder value.

"The belief that shareholders come first is not codified by statute. Rather, it was introduced by a handful of free-market academics in the 1970s and then picked up by business leaders and the media until it became an oft-repeated mantra in the corporate world."

Perhaps ironically, maximizing shareholder value was certainly the underlying foundation in most classes in that MBA program that my grandfather thought was foolish to pursue.

Among today's managers, I don't hear an outright they're-lucky-to-have-a-job philosophy as often as I used to. But what I do hear frequently is the frustration that no one is loyal anymore. And they're right. Their blind spot is that they are only thinking about their employees' attitudes when they complain about disloyalty. In reality, companies aren't loyal either.

A trail of major shifts in employment practices — including more layoffs, moving from defined benefit to defined contribution retirement plans, and the proliferation of non-compete agreements — all sent a strong, clear message to employees from their employers: we're going to take care of ourselves first. The rational response from a smart employee should come as no surprise: I better take care of myself first, too.

So, does the fact that a frontline leader's company puts shareholder value first leave them with an impossible job related to staff engagement and retention? Not at all.

The good news is that the single factor that influences staff engagement most is the boss the employee reports to. What individuals want and need most in their work life is a boss who supports, recognizes, and encourages them. A boss who cares can often overcome the perception of a company that seemingly doesn't.

Given the realities of today's labor market and employees' perception that they need to take care of themselves first, a boss who believes and demonstrates every day that they are lucky to have great individuals working for them has a significant advantage over those leaders who don't get it. And that translates into a work environment that's better for everyone.

3.   Our staff does the real work. I'm here to support them.

No one argues that the stress you carry when you are in charge can be daunting, and it usually only gets more intense as you rise through the leadership ranks of an organization. In addition to the inherent pressures of the job itself, senior leaders carry a sense of personal responsibility with them 24/7 in ways that often feels like the weight of the world is on their shoulders.

So, given the pressures and responsibilities that come with leadership, executives must do the most important work in the company, right? The answer to that question depends on your point of view.

When you are a customer of the company, you know that the most important work of the organization is done by the people on the frontlines. They take care of your needs and make sure the product or service you are receiving is of the highest quality.

Great bosses never forget that taking care of the people who take care of the customers is absolutely essential to sustain growth and success.

While this philosophy sounds right and reasonable on paper, the day-to-day reality is that holding a management position can be a pretty heady experience. You've worked hard to get where you are, right? You deserve the respect of the people who are "below" you, right? Staff on the frontlines don't really understand the pressure you're under and what it takes to run this company, right?

The temptation to begin believing that our roles and responsibilities as leaders are so much more important than the people who work for us is real and significant. It's called hubris, and it happens when our sense of pride and self-confidence get blown way out of proportion.

One of the first times I heard the term applied as a threat to leadership effectiveness was in a presentation many years ago by Jim Collins, soon after he wrote the best-sellers *Built to Last* and *Good to Great*. Near the end of a thought-provoking, energizing workshop session with a large group of children's hospital CEOs, he asked us, "What's the greatest threat to each of you and your organizations?"

Most of us were thinking of increased competition, reduced reimbursement, or more government regulations. His answer was *hubris*.

There are plenty of examples where hubris can start to derail a successful career or company trajectory within the c-suite. But elements of hubris also can begin to impact individuals early in their management career and development. A healthy degree of self-confidence, pride, and assuredness are all essential for leadership success, but hubris can begin to take hold not only when these characteristics are exaggerated but also when they are directed solely toward the self rather than in relation to the entire hardworking team. In other words, great bosses exude confidence in the skills and experience of their team, not just in themselves. They are proud of the collective accomplishments of their team and share that sense of pride with others inside and outside of the company. Assuredness in their staff builds a strong foundation of trust that is key for teams to work well together and achieve maximum success.

Empathy is a wonderful human characteristic that improves our relationships with others in work and in life. It also is an essential characteristic for great bosses. Recognizing the pressures and stress that members of our team face every day helps us better support them; it also helps us as leaders keep our own challenges in perspective.

4.   I take pride and satisfaction in recognizing great work in others and helping them consistently improve.

If you ask most bosses about giving more feedback to their employees, many will reluctantly admit that it's among the parts of their job that they dread most. That said, most will also admit that they know it is an important part of being an effective leader. So, for many, feedback is a necessary evil.

The best bosses have moved beyond viewing feedback as something they dread. Their experience giving feedback is quite the opposite: feedback to team members is one of the most gratifying, consequential, even joyful, parts of their job leading other people. How and why do different bosses view their role in giving feedback so differently?

First, better bosses recognize that "feedback" is a neutral, not a negative, term. Effective feedback can and should be both positive (to reinforce and encourage strong, beneficial behaviors) and negative (to consistently change problem behaviors).

We think of and refer to positive feedback more commonly as recognition or praise. These positive expressions, when shared sincerely and authentically, should be fulfilling and gratifying for both the message deliverer and receiver.

Unfortunately, bad bosses can see the delivery of even positive feedback as a burden rather than a personally gratifying opportunity.

"So, you want me to thank people all the time just for doing their jobs," we occasionally hear. Whether stated or quietly, be-grudgingly believed, that reaction and mindset is at the heart of the old-school "you're lucky to have a job" mentality.

When asked that question, my answer is, "no" ... and "yes."

No, because it is not necessary nor a good idea to thank people for doing the standard, minimal requirements of their job: clocking in on time, being respectful to their co-workers and customers, and completing required reports and paperwork. When we overly recognize routine responsibilities, we can inadvertently send the message that "average" is "exceptional" and lower the performance bar for everyone.

But, yes, there is mutual benefit in recognizing contributions that go beyond routine responsibilities. Don't wait for the life-changing, earth-shattering, over-the-top acts that qualify for the "feel good" human interest stories at the end of the network evening news. When a customer or client takes the time and the effort to call out great service, for example, don't miss the opportunity to make an employee's day by sharing what that customer said, along with a sincere thank you of your own. Sharing that gratitude will make your day better, too.

5. People skills are the heart of my job, not a nice-to-have extra.

"Soft" is an often-used descriptor for individual skills that are not technical, analytical, or scientific. While the phrase soft skills is common, it's a terrible way to describe the important competencies that define the way we interact with and relate to other people.

Just look at a few of the definitions you'll find when you look up "soft:"

- ► Easy; involving little effort
- ► Sentimental or flowery
- ► Not strong or robust
- ► Lenient, permissive, or conciliatory

All these definitions either vastly under value or blatantly contradict critical aspects of strong interpersonal communication and people skills.

One clever phrase and sound piece of advice I've heard that does hit the mark is "soft skills are the hard skills." Sure, there are a few fortunate individuals who are naturally gifted communicators. But for most of us, we hone our people skills when we intentionally pay attention to getting better at the way to connect with others.

This need to focus on personal improvement is especially important for effective leadership communication competencies.

Beyond the foundational skills and practices that help us interact with any other fellow human being, great bosses must be adept at a higher level of communication dexterity, including:

- ► Influencing
- ► Constructive debate
- ► Oral presentation
- ► Facilitation of group conversation
- ► Conflict resolution

The best bosses are intellectually and emotionally aware of their communication strengths and weaknesses. They use this understanding to prioritize development of the people skills they need to be most successful — and to help their team be most successful, as well.

6.   I shouldn't be their friend, but I can't be seen as the enemy.

One of the first pieces of advice I remember receiving when I became a supervisor was, "Your goal should not be to become their friend." While that sound advice is well documented in leadership theory, the issue arises when bosses take the I'm-not-their-friend philosophy too far and assume it's not a problem when employees consider them the enemy.

I experienced first-hand how this exaggerated, warped view of leadership can backfire even before I landed my first full-time job. Working on the high school newspaper was not a paid job, but the staff organization certainly had all the characteristics of a well-functioning company: hierarchy, clearly defined roles and responsibilities, deadlines, and strong teamwork needed to produce a high-quality final product.

A newly named editor-in-chief, who was an extremely smart guy and personal friend, wanted desperately to be a strong, results-focused leader and improve the overall quality of the newspaper. He was a voracious reader and had come across the military maxim that leaders cannot and should not be friends with their subordinates. Unfortunately, his hard-nosed approach and harshly delivered criticism resulted in members of the staff feeling demeaned, insulted, and unappreciated. Almost overnight, a smart, well-intentioned, hard-working guy became a real jerk. Things only got better when several of us and the faculty adviser sat him down to tell him he was going to have a mutiny on his hands if he didn't change his approach. To his credit, he took the advice to heart and changed his ways.

In large companies, managers seldom confront a mass mutiny. Rather, when employees feel unheard, under-appreciated, and demotivated, their leader becomes the victim of slow, painful, mini mutinies, commonly called resignations.

Not being your employees' best friend doesn't mean that you shouldn't care about them as individuals. The line between being friendly and being their friend is one that great bosses learn to walk deftly to develop a strong, supportive, professional relationship with each member of their team.

7. Taking care of others starts with taking care of myself.

When you feel the weight of the world on your shoulders and internalize President Harry Truman's philosophy that "the buck stops here," it is easy to become obsessed with taking care of others and ignore your own personal well-being. That hurts you. And ultimately it hurts your team.

When you're feeling mounting pressure and stress as the boss, there are specific ways to build personal resilience that can help you proactively weather the storm and be at your personal best. That starts with investing in your physical and mental health by following practices that we all know are smart ... but that we sometimes neglect. I've found the following deceptively simple but extremely powerful habits are essential:

- ► Eat right.
- ► Drink less alcohol.
- ► Exercise.
- ► Get a good night's sleep every night.
- ► Nurture important relationships with family and friends.
- ► Challenge your brain with non-work stuff (like Wordle!).

These practices lay a solid foundation. But developing the kind of resilience that better bosses need to be successful goes well beyond these basics. That's why I've devoted an entire chapter to the topic of resilience.

CHAPTER 3

Great Bosses Must be Great Communicators

Better bosses come in many different shapes and sizes, so to speak. Some are natural extroverts and most comfortable interacting with others because that's how they draw energy and inspiration. Others are more introverted, preferring to work through issues methodically on their own before sharing their ideas with their teams. Some are gifted orators and thrive on sharing new ideas "on stage" to internal and external audiences, while others dread the idea of big presentations and struggle with stage fright.

All bosses have their own unique strengths and weaknesses. But all great bosses share one strength in common: they are all great interpersonal communicators. Other leadership traits can be lacking or even absent, but effective communication skills and practices are essential because in many ways they define what makes a leader a great boss.

Effective bosses build strong relationships with their teams in ways that help them feel heard and their ideas valued. They lean into the why behind important decisions, especially the ones that may not be expected or popular. And they provide feedback to help individuals succeed and improve, even when that constructive criticism may be difficult for the boss to share and for employees to hear. All these critical practices rely on superior communication skills.

Sometimes I hear individuals fret over the fact that they're not a "good communicator" because they struggle with public speaking or presenting their ideas convincingly in large groups. And while a healthy degree of self-awareness and reflection is a wonderful characteristic of better bosses, it's not helpful when we're beating ourselves up over the wrong things. When it comes to being a better people-centric leader, we often think about what constitutes great communication in the wrong way. I recognize this problem because that's exactly what I did early in my career.

In school, I learned that I was more comfortable getting up in front of people to speak than many of my classmates. I have to admit that I sort of liked the spotlight. I was good at stringing together words and ideas in ways that sounded convincing, so I got the opportunity to do it more often. Like any skill, the more I practiced, the better I got. And the better I got, the more I heard affirmational feedback: "You know, you look really comfortable in front of an audience. You're a great speaker."

So, what's the problem? I equated being a good public speaker with being a good communicator. Don't misunderstand;

having a strong presence in front of both internal and external audiences is a valuable professional quality, especially for more senior leaders who serve as spokespeople for their companies. But those abilities don't always translate to the type of effective communication employees need from their boss. In fact, if you are too polished, too eloquent, and appear too scripted in interpersonal communication, it can come across as insincere, artificial — even manipulative.

My problem as a communicator was that I often wasn't a very good listener. It wasn't that I didn't care about what other people were feeling or thinking. Rather, I'm easily distracted, and my brain sometimes feels like a pinball machine, constantly bouncing from one idea to another. That can be a wonderful trait to foster innovation and generate a constant stream of fresh ideas. It's a terrible trait when one of your employees needs your undivided attention to discuss an important issue.

I was fortunate that early in my career as a young boss, people that I respected helped me see this major leadership blind spot. My takeaway: in addition to continuing to hone my speaking skills, I desperately needed to work on my listening skills. And that proved to be a much more daunting challenge than I expected.

Listening—I mean *really* listening—is hard work. Especially for busy bosses who are pulled in so many different, often competing, directions. It requires resisting the strong urge to be thinking about the next problem and how we're going to respond instead of thinking through and understanding all aspects of our employee's messages — both spoken and unspoken.

Expanding our view of what constitutes good communication

Communication is one of the most elemental, essential skills we develop early in life. Those first few simple utterances — ma-ma … da-da … wa-wa — put the basics of life at an 18-month-old's beck and call.

But communication is more complicated than simply voicing words. Even the toddler understands at a basic level that if spoken words do not elicit the desired result, then nothing has been communicated. That predicament is often followed by an outburst of crying designed to produce the food, water or favorite toy that was sought in the first place.

How often do we as adults react in a similar fashion? While most of us have learned to control our emotions better than the toddler, failure to communicate can result in responses — raised voice, sharp words, scowled brow, or the "silent treatment" — that only further inhibit the ability to be understood and to build relationships.

Failure to effectively communicate certainly impacts our personal lives. But the problem of not being understood — and not understanding — is a major contributing factor to whether employees feel like they work for a good vs. bad boss.

So, defining what we mean by "communication" is essential before digging deeper into what makes it effective.

Webster's dictionary includes among its definitions for communication: "a process by which information is exchanged between individuals through a common system of symbols, signs or information." Several important words and ideas in this definition help us develop a more comprehensive, useful notion of communication.

First, the definition starts with the foundational concept that communication is a *process*, not an event or single occurrence. Process suggests that communication is more than just a series of unconnected happenings, but instead a structured set of actions that lead to a specific goal. In other words, processes are purposeful, with individual steps designed to achieve a specific result.

Second, the idea that the process is an *exchange* suggests that communication is a two-way street. Unlike some processes that are dependent only on the "executor" of individual steps to achieve success, communication relies on the interplay between sender and receiver of messages. In this sense, successful communication is much like a well-played game of chess. The most adept player pays as much attention to the actions of her opponent as to her own moves to be successful.

Finally, the assumption that the exchange process relies on a *common system of signs, symbols, and information* is key. Expressed more simply, people need to be speaking the same "language" to communicate successfully. In today's diverse, complicated society, language of course refers to more than simply one's native tongue. The commonly expressed complaint, "I just don't get where you're coming from," succinctly captures the challenge many experience in communicating well with others.

When all the requisite conditions are present, communication occurs accurately and predictably. But in the real world, how often do all these conditions exist in any conversation? Too often, what we call "communication" is not at all a process or exchange, but instead the delivery of a message (often electronically) that, for many reasons, isn't accurately received.

It's clear that the ideal conditions outlined in Webster's

definition of communication seldom, if ever, exist in the real world. To compensate for less than perfect conditions, we need to add another critical idea to our concept of what constitutes communication: understanding. Unless our audience both receives *and* fully understands the message we're trying to convey, no real communication has occurred. The same goes for our understanding of messages and ideas others are trying to convey to us.

Focusing on the first two key concepts in our definition — process and exchange — helps the best bosses overcome the problems inherent in communication when our staff don't share common experiences, feelings, and/or knowledge. Additionally, it's helpful to have a structured, intentional framework that formalizes the elements of process and exchange to achieve understanding in all our communication.

The C.A.R.E. model for improving communication

Because communication occurs in so many different circumstances and for so many different reasons, each situation is to some degree unique. That said, there are common principles and approaches that can make any communication encounter more productive, constructive and beneficial for both the message sender and receiver. When applied as a general framework, this approach can be used whether the information you want to convey is technical, emotional, instructive, or matter-of-fact.

Using the acronym C.A.R.E., this structured way of thinking about communication is easy to remember and, with some practice, straightforward to apply. The four stages of the model are:

Compose
Acknowledge
Respond
Evaluate

Note that the letters represent verbs because they describe specific actions you should take to make communication with others more effective, whether you are initiating the conversation or receiving another person's message.

As you apply the elements of the C.A.R.E. model to improve your communication as a boss or in your everyday interactions with family and friends, remember that it provides a conceptual framework for thinking about the most important elements of interpersonal communication. C.A.R.E. is not meant to be a linear, step-by-step checklist. Seldom will you start with the "compose" techniques, then move sequentially through each phase of the model. Depending on the nature of the subject and what you are trying to accomplish in the exchange, it is more likely that you will weave in-and-out of the individual stages as the conversation progresses.

For example, you'll apply the concepts of "compose" to begin a conversation purposely, use "acknowledge" techniques to ensure your ideas are understood, then "evaluate" how well the message receiver is understanding and buying into your ideas. We often return to "acknowledge" for clarification on ideas the other person has shared from their own experience, then use "respond" to address new points of difference or objection.

Active listening is essential at every stage in the model, both to help you determine how well your message is getting through and to appropriately respond to the other person. Like the chess analogy we used earlier, it's impossible to prospectively plan every step of any conversation because you never know exactly how the other person will interpret your information and respond.

The following examples of two versions of a conversation in a busy commercial loan department illustrate how poor communication exacerbates problems and good communication helps fix them.

Jeff Fitzpatrick, a loan officer for Second Community Bank, came flying through the door of the office suite at 9:18 a.m., over 45 minutes later than he or his staff expected.

"Mr. Fairbanks arrived late for our breakfast meeting this morning—as usual—and I didn't think he'd ever stop talking," he complained. "Also as usual," he muttered under his breath.

"He's a nice guy and a great client, but you can't get him to shut up," Jeff went on. "I'm not even sure that I could tell you what he kept going on about because the whole time I was focused on my meeting with the Central Manufacturing CFO Sharon Wilkes coming up at 9:30. We do have everything ready for her, right? This new loan could be the biggest one we close this quarter."

Jeff's right-hand assistant Ellen replied, "Well, yes, I think so. We agreed on a three-year term at 6.25%, with no additional collateral requirement given her relationship with the bank. I have everything ...."

"Wait. No collateral requirements!" Jeff blasted back. "Central Manufacturing is a good client, but the underwriting committee is never going to agree to a loan of this size without additional collateral. Why did you assume that?"

Ellen was sure Jeff had never mentioned the issue of additional collateral, but she knew getting into an argument now would be unproductive. She and other members of the lending team often had to fill in the blanks when Jeff was in overdrive to close additional pieces of business, neglecting to share key details along the way.

"By the way, don't forget that we added a meeting with Bill Manor at 11 a.m. to discuss some concerns he has about how tariffs will affect his sales next quarter," Jim, another member of the department, piped in.

"What?" Jeff asked, in a surprised and frustrated tone. "He was behind on payments earlier this year because of softness in sales, right? Why did this appear on my calendar at the last minute?" I can't be ready for a discussion like that without some additional background.

To save Jim, Ellen bravely stepped in. "Actually, Bill scheduled the meeting last week. We thought it was a good sign that he was coming to us proactively. Remember, we mentioned the meeting to you last Thursday."

"Whatever," Jeff said. "I'm going into the meeting with Ms. Wilkes right now. We'll talk about Bill Manor later. Come on, Ellen, let's go."

Jeff's team was always amazed at how well he could pull things together at the last minute, appearing calm and collected to clients. After a few pleasantries, Jeff started to review the details of the proposed loan.

"So, we're looking at a three-year repayment schedule at a rate of ...."

"Stop right there," Ms. Wilkes interrupted. "I know we talked about different amortization schedules, but I'm sure we agreed on a five-year term. There's no way I'm ready to agree to a term that would stretch us way too far on monthly payments."

Jeff knew that a five-year term was a whole new ballgame that would change every other aspect of the loan, not the least of which was the interest rate.

It was starting to look like this week was not going to be nearly as smooth and successful as he expected.

Jeff was clearly going to have a rough day, and that was largely because of his poor communication, both in the moment and in the days leading up to this conversation. Beyond not providing clear direction, Jeff didn't listen. In turn, that led to incomplete or inaccurate responses to his team's and client's questions and issues.

While there were multiple conversations leading up to the one in his office this morning that were part of the problem, the following scenario focuses on how Jeff could have used the C.A.R.E. model to significantly improve the outcome of his client meetings that day. Where and how the elements of C.A.R.E. are leveraged are noted in **bold.**

Jeff Fitzpatrick, a loan officer for Second Community Bank, came through the door of the office suite at 9:18 a.m., over 45 minutes later than he or his staff expected. But he was ready to focus on the key client meetings in front of him so they would be successful.

"Ellen and Jim, let's circle for a few minutes to review the meetings coming up with Sharon Wilkes and Bill Manor. We've got a little time between the two meetings, so let's focus just on the Central Manufacturing loan first, Jeff explained calmly but with a clear, healthy sense of urgency in his voice. **(Compose: making sure everyone on the team was on the same page and focused on the most immediate issues.)**

Jeff continued, "Ellen, tell me where we are on the details of the loan structure and where there are outstanding questions." **(Acknowledge: focused on highlighting the key aspects of the loan, then using active listening and leading questions to uncover key issues.)**

"So overall, we agreed on a three-year term at 6.25%, with no additional collateral requirement given her relationship with the bank," Ellen explained.

"Let's stop right there," Jeff respectfully interrupted. "I know we talked about options for a three- or five-year term, but my last conversation with Sharon indicated they were leaning heavily toward the five-year option. Can we rerun those numbers at a 6.5% rate to reflect that change?

"We can if we jump on it right now," Ellen reassured. "Jim, please go find Sara and rerun the repayment schedule on a

five-year term. We may not have it right at 9:30, but you can let Ms. Wilkes know that we're making some final adjustments. We'll bring it to you as soon as possible during the meeting." **(Respond: answering the problem of the wrong loan term and proposing a viable solution.)**

"Great," Jeff said. "Now let's talk through this additional collateral issue. First, I know the underwriting committee is never going to approve a loan of this size without some additional protection to reduce our risk. Ellen, did you or any other member of the team promise this?" **(Acknowledge: refocusing the conversation on the next key issue to uncover problems and agree on a solution.)**

"Absolutely not," Ellen assured. "We just assumed we'd waive additional requirements like we did on their last loan. But I clearly see why this is different."

"Well, that's good news," Jeff said, with a sigh of relief. "I'll have to begin that conversation with Sharon this morning, and it would be helpful to have a list of the assets we've tapped as collateral over the past five years. Can another member of your team pull that?" **(Respond: clearly explaining what needs to happen next on this issue.)**

Ellen immediately replied, "I know exactly where that information is. I'll take this one myself. But before I do, is there anything else we need to cover before that meeting starts?" **(Evaluate: prompting the need to wrap up the conversation, ensuring that all key issues had been covered.)**

"Nope," Jeff gratefully expressed. "We're good. Just stand by because there's a good chance other questions may come up in the meeting that your team may be able to address quickly."

"Thanks, everybody," Jeff said as he started to walk toward the lobby to greet Sharon. "I'm feeling good about how this business is going to boost our fourth-quarter results."

Remember that the goal of the model is to make communication clearer and effective, not more complicated. Collectively, the techniques in the C.A.R.E. model are designed to:

- ► Assure understanding,
- ► Focus our communication and attention,
- ► Respond thoughtfully, and
- ► Help us evaluate the effectiveness of our communication and its impact on others.

Starting strong makes all communication more effective

All components of the C.A.R.E. model work together to make interactions with others more efficient, beneficial, and rewarding. But the foundational stage — compose — arguably is most crucial. Without a deliberate, purposefully start to a conversation, the other phases of the C.A.R.E. model simply don't work as well.

Knowing where you're going before you begin seems like common sense. But how often do we wander into important conversations without a clear idea of exactly what we want to accomplish or what we need the other person we're talking with to do. The pace of life in general — especially for bosses — makes the need for clear, purposeful communication even more critical.

Unfortunately, as the complexity of our jobs as leaders increases, we tend to plan less, not more. "How can I possibly stop to think when I have so many issues competing for my time and attention," is a common belief and challenge during times of stress and overload. While forging ahead without a clear idea of where we're going may seem to save time in the moment, an unfocused approach usually wastes time in the long-run. Not being present also impacts our relationships with members of our team.

Even if you accept the philosophy that beginning conversations clearly and with purpose is the best approach, you may still question how you can possibly be collected and composed given the constant state of chaos around you. Following are tips to help you adjust your mindset to achieve communication effectiveness from the start of a conversation.

> *Quickly think about what you want and need to get out of a conversation before you begin.*

This simple practice is obviously important for a speaker to structure ideas in a concise, understandable way. But the approach has advantages for the listener as well. Thinking about the purpose and outcome of the conversation helps both message sender and receiver focus on the specific issue at hand rather than other things vying for attention. Unless a conversation is scheduled and meant to cover complex or sensitive issues, the process of thinking about the results you need from an exchange should only take a few seconds.

Focus on one issue at a time.

There are few times when a boss has the luxury of being concerned about only one problem or task. But trying to solve multiple problems and answer many questions simultaneously is both inefficient and ineffective. While multi-tasking may be en vogue, it is a dangerous practice when communicating important information to another human being. Science tells us that if we believe our brain is multi-tasking, we're kidding ourselves.[7] Rather, the brain bounces from one single thought or idea to the next, often in rapid-fire fashion. Smart communicators anticipate and plan for covering multiple issues intentionally and sequentially rather than randomly reacting and getting distracted like Dug the dog in the movie *Up*: "Squirrel!"

Call the other person by name.

Saying another person's name has psychological benefits for both the sender and receiver of messages. For the sender, it serves as a little cue to your brain to stay focused on this conversation with the intended receiver. And for the listener, it is an unmistakable signal that the message is important enough for the speaker to have singled you out and recognized you in a personal way.

Sit down.

In focus group research, patients and family members in healthcare settings consistently mentioned how much they valued a caregiver sitting down to share and receive information, even if it was only for a few moments. The research reveals that individuals perceive that the doctor or nurse has spent longer with them when they sit down than when they are standing.

No physical action more strongly signals that a person is really focused on listening and responding thoughtfully than sitting down. Bosses who are constantly running from one crisis to the next convey a clear message of respect to employees when they sit down to talk with them.

When you can't sit down physically, think about sitting down mentally. In other words, anchor yourself to one spot so that you can really listen and respond appropriately to another person's thoughts.

Look at the other person.

While this suggestion may seem basic, there is nothing quite so centering as looking another human being in the eye when communicating. With constant technological distractions, it is easy to glance at your phone, a tablet, or your watch, and as a result not focus on the important conversation at hand. This problem plagues both receivers and senders of interpersonal messages.

What about phone or electronic conversations via instant messaging? It's helpful to mentally picture the person at the other end of the phone call or text screen in their environment as a way to stay focused both on the individual and their possible reactions to your message.

Take a deep, cleansing breath to recenter.

Being a great boss includes the ability to have difficult conversations in a respectful, rational, calm way. That starts with entering these conversations in the right state of mind. When you feel overly anxious going into a conversation, that stress is tough to hide. It can actually cause the other person to mirror your emotions and make the interaction even more difficult than it has to be.

A deep, cleansing, recentering breath can help. Rather than obsessing over the worst case scenario, picture the best possible outcome for the conversation given the circumstances. That helps us enter the conversation with a more balanced, non-judgmental attitude. When your employee sees that attitude, their level of stress and even aggression may moderate, too.

The role of better communication in building trust

Up to this point, we've explored primarily the factors that influence communication effectiveness at the actual point of information exchange. But laying groundwork before a message is ever conveyed can be just as critical to achieving connection and understanding.

To appreciate why laying a solid foundation with another person is so important in the communication process, think about "planting" your message or idea in the same way the gardener might sow seeds. While a blooming flower or plump vegetable is the ultimate goal, the smart gardener knows that the way he prepares the soil is the most important determinant of how healthy the plant will eventually be. Seeds thrown onto rocky, dry, infertile soil usually don't take root. And those seeds that do sprout will have little chance of surviving any type of adverse conditions or challenge.

The same is true of the messages, ideas, information, and opinions we attempt to plant in others' minds through communication. Especially when our message is complex or contentious, planting ideas without establishing trust and rapport is akin to the gardener wastefully throwing out seeds on dry, rocky soil.

Investing in rapport yields better understanding

While it is easy to recognize that rapport helps facilitate effective communication and ultimate understanding, defining and achieving rapport are complicated. Many factors go into what we think of as "rapport:" shared experiences and backgrounds, common goals and aspirations, like personalities, or even a similar sense of humor. But by far the most critical component of rapport from the communication standpoint is trust. Perhaps no other condition hinders effective communication more than mistrust between the sender and receiver of a message. This is especially true for the relationship between a boss and their staff.

In building a better understanding of what defines and influences rapport, it's important first to recognize that it is not a static state. Many gain a false sense of confidence by assuming that rapport developed with another person or employee exists forever and can always be relied upon. In fact, both external forces and our every action can influence the level of trust and rapport we enjoy with an individual.

If we think about our actions toward others as investments in building strong rapport, the state of goodwill we achieve performs very much like a savings account. During good, prosperous times, we make deposits in our account that we know we may have to draw upon during a rainy day. The more we invest in the account, the greater our level of confidence and comfort that we can live through unexpected challenges in bad times.

Rapport works in largely the same way. From the moment we meet another human being and begin interacting with them, we start building a rapport account, of sorts, that we are constantly either contributing to or withdrawing from. Actions that are honest, constructive, supportive and trust-building increase our balance, while those that cause others to question our motives or actions decrease the level of rapport we've worked to establish.

But the balance in our investment account is dependent on more than just our own deposits and withdrawals. As everyone with a retirement account experiences during a decline in the stock market, our account balance can drop dramatically without us making any withdrawals at all.

Like our retirement account, there are outside factors at work that positively or negatively influence the way a team feels about their boss. The fact that we have little control over external forces emphasizes the need for us to pay close attention to and nurture those factors that we can influence. Simply, we need to be making positive deposits in our rapport account with others as frequently as possible.

Why is rapport so important?

From the moment we meet another person, we begin a process of instinctive, informal evaluation that determines the degree to which we feel comfortable and connected to them. Sometimes this process begins even before we meet someone in person through their resume or comments we hear from a colleague who knows them.

Because the informal evaluation process begins so quickly and unconsciously, first impressions are especially important. Often within seconds of seeing a new employee and initiating a conversation, we have begun thinking about whether we can trust them. Of course, they are making the same assessment and judgments about us as their new boss.

Building lasting rapport

While creating a good first impression is important, it is only a small first step in building long-term rapport with a team member with whom we'll hopefully interact for many years to come. Here, rapport is a constantly evolving state that is influenced by what we say, how we say it, and actions we take.

The following are suggestions to consider when your goal is to build long-term, sustainable rapport with your team. Few, if any, of these recommendations will surprise, but each seemingly simple idea carries enormous power to strengthen rapport and incrementally improve the way we communicate with others.

1.   Show a sincere interest in issues and concerns of others.

To establish trust, others have to know that they can count on us to listen, understand, and offer advice on subjects that are particularly important to them. Acknowledging and learning more about problems and challenges that are important to your team is critical to building rapport, even when they may be issues we can't immediately solve or even influence. Again, active listening is the most essential skill in showing sincere interest and concern when an employee needs your perspective and advice. While ultimately they may be seeking your opinion, attempt to listen first with as open a mind as possible so that you can truly understand all of the aspects of the problem before stating your thoughts and ideas.

2.   Develop a spirit of cooperation and willingness to compromise.

Active listening and understanding does not mean that you can or even should agree with everything others say to you. It does, however, mean that you are receptive to hearing and understanding their ideas before jumping to your own conclusions. Co-workers who come to know you as someone who is open to listening and trying to understand diverse ideas will be more apt to reach out and open up. Similarly, your openness will engender a willingness among others to consider your opinions and ideas thoughtfully and fairly.

3.   Learn to disagree constructively.

Disagreement is both a reality and an important part of effective communication between individuals or groups. Opposing ideas shared constructively almost always lead to a better understanding of the issues, as well as a final solution that's better than the one initially suggested by either side. But disagreement also has the potential to erode rapport and shut down interaction between a leader and her team if not handled constructively. Effective communicators learn to respectfully acknowledge other's ideas and positions before sharing their own points of view.

4. Look beyond your own biases and pre-conceived ideas.

Especially when considering a topic you feel strongly about, the ability to honestly evaluate others' ideas and information is an essential skill in building long-term rapport. Bias exists in many forms and for many reasons. While people usually equate bias with narrow-minded, unfair, prejudicial thinking, bias can be both well-supported and rational. As long as our biases categorize *ideas* and not *people*, they are often acceptable and defendable.

We can't just get rid of our biases outright, but we can make a conscious effort to set them aside when we're evaluating new ideas. How often do colleagues jump to conclusions that a new approach or idea will not work because "we've always done it another way." An inability to look beyond conventional thinking not only stifles creativity and new solutions, but also can stifle rapport with our team.

5. Be genuinely — but respectfully — honest.

This final recommendation may sound simplistic, but honesty and integrity are at the heart of building effective personal and professional relationships. This doesn't necessarily mean that you should share everything you know on a particular topic with everyone you are communicating with. It does mean, however, that when you are presented with a straightforward, reasonable question regarding a subject, you will answer truthfully. This truthfulness may take the form of an admission that there are certain facts or data that you cannot share because of confidentiality.

Ultimately, rapport with other human beings can be a fragile state that must be consistently monitored and nurtured. An appreciation that each word you speak can influence your future ability to communicate openly and effectively with your team is the first step in using rapport to your advantage in both your professional and personal life.

CHAPTER 4

The Connection Between Bad Bosses and Burnout

During the pandemic, a new vocabulary emerged to describe the plight of employees and their reactions to the stress of this uncertain time. From "the Great Resignation" to "quiet quitting," social scientists, the media, and management experts created clever descriptors to capture unprecedented labor market changes and challenges. But perhaps the most common term we heard to describe employees' emotional, mental, and physical reaction to the stress of COVID-19 was neither new nor novel: burnout.

While burnout was exacerbated by the extraordinary conditions during the pandemic, the problem had been described many years earlier by American psychologist Herbert Freudenberger in the 1970s.[8] Originally, Freudenberger coined the term to describe the consequences of severe stress and high ideals of "helping" professions. For example, doctors, nurses, and teachers can reach an unhealthy degree of self-sacrifice for others and become exhausted, cynical, and less able to cope. Today, the term has been broadened to apply to anyone whose self-sacrifice crosses the line into an unhealthy, unsustainable state.

The symptoms of burnout are well-documented and usually apparent to co-workers and family:

- ► **Exhaustion** (physical and emotional)
- ► **Cynicism** (dramatic swings in attitude overall)
- ► **Inefficacy** (loss of sense of personal effectiveness despite working harder)

In addition to these originally described symptoms, many experts have added *depersonalization,* which is largely a coping mechanism for the first three symptoms. Simply, people stop caring as much as they once did.

A natural response to the symptoms of burnout has been to step-up employee wellness strategies and programs. Ranging from traditional mental health services to mindfulness apps and classes, these efforts are well intentioned but have fallen short of the goal of significantly reducing burnout. Beyond the question of whether or not they are effective, there's a bigger problem: they ignore the underlying things companies do — either deliberately for survival or unintentionally — that their employees know are contributing to burnout.

Two conversations coming out of the pandemic with experienced, accomplished professionals for whom I have a great deal of respect helped me really understand the magnitude of the treat-the-symptoms problem.

The first conversation was with a seasoned, highly regarded chief nursing officer. During a wide-ranging conversation about long-term implications of the pandemic for the health care workforce, I asked her about efforts to help employees become more resilient.

"Frankly, I find it offensive," she replied bluntly. "Frontline caregivers are working harder and are being stretched further than ever before during an unprecedented crisis, and we're telling them they should be more resilient? Their heroic responses to unbelievable challenges facing our organizations and patients look pretty damn resilient to me."

Another similar conversation with a senior leader in another company focused on the indirect message we send to employees when we only deal with symptoms and coping mechanisms.

"I think the message we're sending when we only talk about helping employees improve well-being is that it really sucks to work here ... and it's not going to get any better," she said matter-of-factly. "So, we're going to provide some meditation and mindfulness training to help you cope with it."

Both of these reflections from experienced leaders convinced me that it is not only frontline staff who are struggling with burnout, but also the people they report to. Conscientious bosses, especially in careers defined by a high degree of self-sacrifice such as health care, education, and law enforcement, are concerned and thoughtfully considering the work environment we create not just in individual companies but across entire industries. Given the inordinate impact that bosses have on the engagement and experience of frontline staff, how to better develop, support and reward managers becomes a top work environment improvement priority.

Experts in performance improvement methodologies across industries share the belief that making progress in work teams, companies, or across an industry starts with understanding the foundational root causes of the issues that are ineffective, inefficient, or just plain broken.

While many talk about burnout from personal experience, Christina Maslach, PhD, professor emerita of psychology at University of California Berkeley and author of the book *The Truth About Burnout*,[9] devoted the majority of her career to understanding the condition and what organizations can do to minimize or prevent it. Dr. Maslach's pivotal research over 40+ years provides important insights for organizations, beginning with the need to focus more on underlying root causes than simply high visibility symptoms.

One of the most enlightening and consequential findings that came to light from the research conducted by Dr. Maslach and her colleagues dispels the widely held perception that burnout is simply about too much work. While the quantity and structure of work is indeed one of the major root causes, there are five additional contributing conditions that, depending on the setting and circumstances, can be just as consequential.

The remainder of this chapter is devoted to exploring the six root causes of burnout and the impact that better bosses can and should have on addressing them.

The Work Itself

"Too much" is far too simplistic an explanation for why workload contributes to burnout. Indeed, an unhealthy number of hours of work each week for an extended period affects both physical and mental health. But how much is too much? That depends largely on an individual and the non-work situation and circumstances in their life at any given time. Especially early in their careers, many driven, competitive individuals choose to take on extra shifts, projects — even extra part time jobs — to increase their income and standing in the organization. The extra hours alone seldom trigger burnout.

In most cases, the challenges employees face in their work are structural, not just dependent on the number of hours they're working. When teachers have too many students in their class-room, nurses have too many patients assigned during a shift, or distribution warehouse workers have too many packages to reasonably process, that contributes to burnout. These conditions also can affect quality and safety when they become the standard rather than the exception in a company.

Frontline leaders bear the majority of the immediate burden when these conditions persist. What we hear from managers is that they often self-impose a reluctance to speak up and share their concerns up the ladder for fear of not being seen as a "team player." But the best bosses see advocacy for their employees as a critical part of their role, using available data to describe and quantify the impact inadequate staffing can have on quality, customer service, and employee retention. While great frontline bosses don't throw senior leaders under the bus as an excuse for workload, they also don't abandon all responsibility for the situation and the structure of work in their department long-term.

Strong bosses also partner with their teams to explore ways to take low-value or unnecessary tasks out of the day-to-day routine. Finding and removing inefficiency is at the heart of Lean and Six

Sigma process improvement methodologies, and better bosses embrace this philosophy even if they're not a "black belt" trained expert in more complex statistical analyses. Empowering staff to think about how their work could change and encouraging them to share their ideas is one of the hallmarks of a great boss.

I saw a brilliant example of the power of this philosophy many years ago when I was working with nursing leaders at Ascension Saint Thomas Rutherford Hospital in Murfreesboro, Tennessee. On one busy nursing unit, we were looking for ways to make the work they were already doing translate to better patient experiences and loyalty. Hourly nurse rounding was one of the practices we explored.

Years ago, a nursing research study documented the patient safety advantages of checking in on patients more frequently and intentionally. Out of this study "hourly nurse rounding" was born. For the next decade, the practice became the go-to solution for fixing issues ranging from patient experience scores to staff retention.

If you ask frontline nurses what they think of hourly rounding, you're likely to get wide ranging responses from "it's really helped reduce call light use," to "it's bureaucratic busy work that wastes my time." Whether a team has a positive or negative view of the practice usually traces to how they were involved in — or left out of — its design and implementation plan.

Early in our work with the nursing unit at Saint Thomas Rutherford, I was blown away by their self-initiated, break-through efforts to make hourly rounding work better for both staff and patients. When I asked the group to think about ways that they might prioritize and make hourly rounding tasks more efficient and effective, one team member immediately spoke up.

"You mean like Susan," he said. Of course, my next question was who's Susan and what is she doing differently.

"Susan has this sixth sense about when a patient needs her to come into their room," he explained.

"So, it sounds like Susan is somewhat clairvoyant?" I queried with a smile. "But there must be something Susan is doing that helps her better anticipate her patients' needs."

"There is," he continued. "She's really good about proactively thinking about each different patient that she has responsibility for at the beginning of her shift, then using that understanding of their needs to prioritize how — and how often — she rounds on each patient."

Brilliant, I'm thinking! But before I could pose my next easily anticipated question, he preemptively continued.

"And that's why we developed the D.A.R.N. list," he said. "D.A.R.N. stands for Daily Acuity and Risk Enumeration. We developed a short list of conditions and risks that help us prioritize each patient's needs relative to other patients. A higher D.A.R.N. score might require us to be in a patient's room more often than every hour. And a lower risk score means we won't need to check in on other patients as often, especially during the night."

Again, I'm thinking ... brilliant!

While it might be easy to give all the credit for development and implementation of the D.A.R.N. list to motivated, self-directed staff members who saw an opportunity to improve their work structure and experience for the patients, it is important to note the important role that Annie Sloan, their manager, played. Annie created an environment where staff members felt comfortable speaking up, stepping out, and advancing ideas to improve the work for everyone. Annie was a great boss.

Voice/Control

Since the emergence of Lean, Six Sigma, and similar high-ly-structured performance improvement methodologies, giving employees more voice and control in decision-making has often become an "event." That can be both good and bad. When we lean too heavily into Lean structure and events, we may be missing day-to-day opportunities for individual team members to speak up, ask questions, and suggest solutions that admittedly fall short of a full-blown plan coming out of a Kaizen event. Not every problem warrants the cost, time, and resources required to launch a comprehensive PI committee or task force.

In the case of the D.A.R.N. list described above, the nursing staff took the initiative without any official christening of a PI team because their boss encouraged team members to take control over improving their own work.

Giving up some degree of control can feel like a risky move, especially for a newer manager trying to establish their own credibility and authority. But giving up an appropriate degree of control is something great bosses embrace because they understand it increases trust with their team and can make everyone more successful.

When I reflect on what an appropriate degree of autonomy and measured control looks and feels like, I think back to golf lessons I took many years ago. My curmudgeon of a teacher, who had a single-digit handicap well into his 70s, always had clever analogies and stories to drive home the finer points of the game. The way he described how to grip the club sticks with me even today: "Squeezing the club too tightly is the biggest mistake new golfers make. Grip it gently like you'd hold a small baby bird in your hands. You don't want it to fly away at the wrong time and place, but you also don't want to choke the poor thing, so he never flies again."

In the name of supporting and protecting their teams from failure, bad bosses often hold on too tight, choking the spirit of innovation and willingness to go above-and-beyond out of every member of their staff. Your best and brightest are especially susceptible to burning out when all their autonomy and control is taken away. Over-achievers want to soar, and good bosses appreciate and encourage their spirit and ingenuity.

Can leaders cede too much authority and control? Of course they can, but the line they have to be careful about crossing is never perfectly clear or absolute. Good bosses never abandon their teams and allow them to take on unreasonable risks or inevitable failure. Rather, they learn to test the line between beneficial autonomy and unhealthy gambles, adjusting it based on the circumstances and degree of risk involved if their strategy fails. Also, giving your team more voice does not mean that your voice as a leader must be completely silenced. Better bosses find the right ways to weigh in without choking the excitement and enthusiasm of staff members looking for ways to make things better.

One of the most powerful ways great bosses respond to team members' new ideas is with questions, not absolute statements. For example, you may fear (or given your past experience, confidently know) that a new process is going to take far longer to implement because it will come up against resistance from another department affected by the decision. You may be tempted to blurt out, "This is going to be impossible to implement because that other department will sabotage your work." (By the way, it is important to humbly remember that very good bosses occasionally make very wrong assumptions.)

A much healthier, introspective response leads with questions that respectfully challenge both staff and boss to carefully think through all the risks: *How do you see the actual implementation rolling out? If it takes longer than expected, how will that affect success? How do you think other departments will react? Did you get their input during your assessment and design process?*

When better bosses push themselves and their teams to thoughtfully consider all the potential risks and rewards, that's not taking away control and voice. It's developing and advancing your team's critical thinking skills so the voice they provide and control they assume is smart and effective.

Fairness

Establishing a workplace culture that is "fair" may be the most nuanced challenges great bosses face in building a work environment that is fulfilling and reduces the likelihood of burnout. After all, what is "fair?" The subjective state of fairness looks and feels quite different depending on an employee's background, life experiences, and expectations of the job. There also will likely be significant generational differences in judging fairness.

Focusing on company policies when judging fairness is usually a no-win proposition. It's easy to argue that an organization's absence/tardiness policy or the structure of paid time off (PTO) isn't fair. Similarly, I could argue that the fact my daughter, who is a masters-prepared elementary school teacher, is paid about what a busy Uber driver makes isn't fair. Given the impact she has on young lives, shouldn't she be making more than the person who drives me to the airport? But the Uber driver likely has a different point of view.

In my work with teams, I've found that the perception of a boss's fairness doesn't rely on structural issues but rather centers on two major questions:

- ► How do they hold staff accountable?
- ► How do they communicate decisions?

During our qualitative assessment focus groups with employees in an organization, we always ask, "What happens if you have a lower performer who isn't pulling their weight on your team?" If their answer is "nothing," we know that most members of the team would not describe their work environment as fair.

What most employees — especially star performers — are looking for in a boss is the willingness and ability to hold people equitably accountable for their actions and performance. We often hear individuals share that they are willing and happy to go the extra mile for the team and for their customers. But they are quick to add that when colleagues don't share that same dedication and commitment, it takes much of the joy out of their efforts to provide exceptional service.

Better bosses first set clear, consistent, shared expectations for all members of the team. This helps minimize the excuse that, "I didn't know we were supposed to do it that way."

Second, effective leaders honor and bolster these expectations by providing consistent feedback to individuals on their performance. Better bosses understand that positive feedback, which recognizes and reinforces outstanding actions and contributions, can powerfully influence behaviors across the entire team. People notice when others are being recognized and they aren't.

Better bosses also appreciate the responsibility they have to share constructive criticism with members of the team who fall short of their expectations, leaving their co-workers to pick up the slack.

In addition to holding employees equitably accountable, strong leaders emphasize the "why" in their communication around key decisions, new processes and procedures, or other changes that affect the team, especially those that may be perceived as unfair. Unpopular decisions may still be unpopular, but explaining how the decision was made, factors that were considered, and the rationale supporting the decision means that unwelcome change can still be seen as fair because everyone is impacted similarly.

Recognition

For such a seemingly straightforward concept, recognition can be one of the least understood and poorly implemented strategies to help employees feel less burned out. Smart leaders who effectively recognize strong performance and contributions follow three general tenets:

- ► *Individualized* is always more powerful than *group*
- ► *Frequent/specific* is always more powerful than the *big event*
- ► *From-the-heart* is always more powerful than *from-the-head*

To be most meaningful and impactful, the recipient of recognition has to feel like their boss actually noticed something important they've done that deserves recognition. This concept was driven home for me a few years ago when we were working with a hospital Environmental Services team to improve both employee and patient/customer experience. The housekeeping role involves back-breaking work that is often under-recognized in health care, hospitality, and property management. I've had EVS staff members tell me that they often feel invisible, that no one knows or calls them by their name, and that co-workers from other departments seem to "look right through me."

Early in our project, it was clear that one specific director and her managers in the Environmental Services department really did care and genuinely valued the contributions their team members made every day. They knew them by name and worked hard to create an upbeat, appreciative environment in the department. At the beginning of every shift, they pulled the team together for a high-energy huddle to share key information for that day. The huddle ended with an almost rally-like cheer saying, "You guys are terrific and do a wonderful job. We love you! Have a great day."

I must admit that when I left the first huddle, I was on a high. The leadership team was enthusiastic in their praise and came across as sincerely grateful for the work of the team.

It was a couple of days later that I came to see the limitations of the group pep rally and why some members of the team looked less than excited to be starting their shift. The leadership team's closing message was essentially the same cheerleading-style praise delivered in the same way every day. Since we had spent time in the trenches with members of their team, one of their star employees felt comfortable discreetly pulling me aside at the end of the huddle.

"I don't want you to take this the wrong way," she said up front. "It's nice, I guess, when they tell us we're great and that they love us every day. But what really means something to me is when one of them pulls me aside, looks me in the eye, and says, 'Thank you for what you did for that cancer patient who was down,' or 'we appreciated you staying late last night because we had so many discharges.'"

"I hope that doesn't sound mean," she said, "but I thought you needed to hear that."

Indeed, I did need to hear and understand that, because individualized, sincere recognition is something that great bosses understand and find opportunities to leverage every day.

Community/Teamwork

A work environment characterized by strong, supportive relationships among frontline staff can be a powerful deterrent to individual burnout. It also can be one of the most difficult conditions for a boss to single-handedly build and sustain. Savvy leaders know investing time and energy into creating strong teamwork benefits everyone. Work groups that share a strong sense of community not only are there for one another; they are there for their boss.

A great boss both intentionally creates and then nurtures a positive work community first and foremost by modeling the practices and behaviors they desire in their team. "What they see is what we get" is a catchphrase I repeat often when working with leaders in organizations. If the walk doesn't match the talk, employees will always reflect the actions they see, not the pronouncements you make that teamwork is important.

In a hospital I had just started working with, we asked front-line staff during our assessment phase about the visibility of the senior leadership team and how connected they felt with them. We heard the same story retold several times in different groups we met with throughout the day. Staff shared that when the chief nursing officer joined the hospital executive team, he devoted considerable time to getting to know staff by spending time in individual departments. One nursing unit he visited one evening was beyond busy because patient admissions had spiked, and they were down one staff member. He asked the charge nurse what he could do to help. After he insisted that he really was serious about wanting to help, the charge reluctantly admitted that there was a patient who wanted a bath, and she wasn't sure the staff would be able to get to her that night.

"He actually gave the patient a bath!" one of the nurses in the focus group exclaimed, followed by nods of appreciation from the rest of the group. Clearly, this story had spread like wildfire because everyone was immediately familiar with it.

The impact of the CNO's generous expression of true teamwork, which spanned all levels of the organization, was arguably not the most amazing part of this story. When I heard about the bath for the third time, I asked, "How long ago did this happen? When did your CNO join the organization?" The nurses looked at each other quizzically around the table before someone answered, "Gosh, that must have been four or five years ago." By their expressions you could see that even they were surprised that it happened years ago yet seemed like it was just yesterday.

A servant leader's modeling of true teamwork is enduring and has a powerful cumulative effect on their staff.

As staff begin to clearly understand and reinforce what "community" looks and feels like for their team, recruitment and selection of new team members take on a much higher degree of significance. It is no longer that they want to find the person with the right skills and experience; more importantly, they want to find the person that aligns with their culture of community and teamwork.

A couple of times early in my career I hired someone because of their specific experience, educational pedigree, and exceptional intelligence. In each case, there was a little red flag waving in the distance that caused me to question whether they would be a good fit with the culture of the organization and other members of leadership. Ignoring that little red flag was a mistake. Their inability or unwillingness to bond with and support their colleagues became a liability that was far more disruptive and destructive than I ever imagined it could be.

Staff in the trenches understand how problematic a colleague who doesn't share their commitment to community can be. In a focus group in Birmingham, Alabama, a staff member convinced me just how significant teamwork can — and should — be in terms of engagement and work fulfillment. To the simple question, "Why do you like working here?", she leaned forward in her chair across the table, looked me straight in the eye, and emphatically answered, "I'll tell you why I work here. I work here because I know people have my back. And they know that I have theirs. We're there for one another always, including our manager. She's there for us, and we're there for her."

She went on to explain the importance of new staff joining the team. "We're pretty good at finding people who understand how we roll," she explained. "But every so often, we make a mistake, and someone doesn't get that we backup one another. They end up being really uncomfortable here, and they usually self-select out. And that's OK. If they don't fit and don't understand our teamwork, they're better off working someplace else."

Purpose

Understanding and leveraging purpose in organizations is one of the most talked about issues — and opportunities — in companies today. In Fall 2019, 181 CEOs from the prestigious Business Roundtable signed a new statement on the "Purpose of a Corporation." No longer is simply driving shareholder value the top priority, they said. The statement recognized an organization's role in serving all stakeholders: customers, employees, suppliers, communities, and shareholders.

Many would argue that some industries and companies just inherently have a higher purpose and thus an advantage in helping employees minimize burnout. Not-for-profit and health care providers are good examples. Leaders in these organizations might contend that they have always understood their purpose. After all, can there be a higher purpose than serving fellow human beings when they're in need at some of the most vulnerable times in their lives? But if that's true, why is burnout in health care and many social service organizations so high?

The important consideration for bosses in health care and other industries who want to help their teams connect to purpose is how often they talk about, appreciate, and celebrate that purpose. Recent research and insights into how purpose can and should be leveraged in organizations gives us important things to think about.

"When Work Has Meaning" proclaimed the cover story of the July/August 2018 issue of the Harvard Business Review[10]. Like the remarkable statement from the Business Roundtable, this article turns long-standing business principles and theories on their head. Authors Anjan Thakor and Robert Quinn argue that the "principle-agent model" describing the economic relationship between a company and its employees precludes the notion of a fully engaged workforce.

"People who find meaning in their work don't hoard their energy and dedication," the authors stress. "They give them freely, defying conventional economic assumptions about self-interest. They do more — and they do it better."

The power of purpose doesn't just naturally happen and influence the work environment in organizations, even when that underlying purpose is as mighty as it is in healthcare and other service industries. Leveraging purpose must be intentional, authentic, and central to how work gets done in the organization.

Strong leaders know that *how* a feeling of purpose is internalized and lived by every team member every day is the real test of its effectiveness and ability to engage staff. The organization's values — both formally stated and informally understood — speak most directly to how frontline staff members experience purpose. Unfortunately, most organizations spend lots of time developing the perfect list of values and very little time thinking about how they will meaningfully influence the work environment, customers' experiences, and overall performance.

An inclusive, well-facilitated, collaborative process is the ideal way to elevate and begin to truly live values every day. A "Values

Summit" works when it brings together diverse constituencies from throughout the organization. The key is to define and communicate in meaningful, compelling ways the behaviors that are at the heart of each value and why they are critical to the success of the organization and to the personal success of each and every team member.

One of the most successful, personally gratifying Values Summits I've ever been a part of was with the team at Summa Health in Akron, Ohio. At the time, the organization was going through a jarring senior leadership transition. Many longtime staff members questioned whether the organization that they thought they knew well had lost its way. Refocusing on the core values that were part of Summa's historically collaborative culture was a critical part of an overall plan to reengage staff at every level.

The Values Summit pulled together about 25 individuals from every level of the organization ... with one exception; no senior leaders were part of the initial brainstorming and crafting process. We wanted to hear from the people on the frontlines of serving customers, which included doctors, housekeepers, security guards, nurses, receptionists — and every imaginable position in between. By design, these individuals were not selected randomly. The group was composed of Summa's "stars," the people who represented the very best of the organization and who understood at heart the enduring values that made Summa a special place.

Over the course of an afternoon and following morning, that group created an inspiring statement that they named "Our Commitments:"

Serve with passion.

- *Appreciate the privilege we have every day to serve our fellow man at some of the most vulnerable times in their lives ... when they are sick, injured, frightened and in pain.*

- *Look for the joy in our work, paying attention to the impact each of us can have in others' lives.*

- *Serve with integrity by always following through on commitments, being honest and acting ethically.*

- *Create a welcoming environment by always making eye contact and greeting others we pass in hallways and elevators.*

- *Recognize and celebrate what's right about Summa Health while always looking for opportunities to make the care we provide even better.*

- *Go above and beyond.*

Personalize care.

- *Empower patients and family members to be involved in decisions related to their care.*

- *Communicate openly and effectively with patients and their family members, encouraging them to share their thoughts, concerns and questions.*

- *Make eye contact.*

- *Encourage patients and family members to share their questions and concerns by asking open-ended questions like, "How can I help you most right now?"*

▶ *Listen actively and ensure understanding by paraphrasing back what the patient has just told you.*

▶ *Always knock and ask the patient if it is all right to enter their room.*

▶ *Call patients by their preferred name each time you enter their room.*

▶ *Introduce yourself by name and explain your role on the care team to patients and family members.*

▶ *Improve the continuity of care by always helping the patient know and understand what comes next during their visit or stay.*

Value every person.

▶ *Look for the best in every individual we serve and in those we serve with.*

▶ *Treat others without bias or judgment; we have not walked in their shoes.*

▶ *Respect and celebrate the diversity of the patients we serve and the talented colleagues we work with every day.*

▶ *Treat others with courtesy and respect, even when we may disagree with their ideas.*

▶ *Recognize the talents of others on our team, expressing thanks for their contributions.*

▶ *Offer a friendly ear to colleagues who may be struggling. Be willing to reach out to others when you need help or are having a bad day.*

Take ownership.

► *Role model the actions and qualities that you seek in others.*

► *Beyond just identifying the problem, be part of the solution in any situation.*

► *Even when a solution seems like the right one, continue to evaluate it and make changes to improve outcomes.*

► *Be aware of your own emotions and the ways they may affect how others react to you.*

► *To insure a safe environment for patients and colleagues, always follow "I'm 4 Safety" behaviors.*

► *Advocate for the patient and his/her expressed needs.*

Work collaboratively.

► *Encourage patients, family members and colleagues to speak up when they have a concern by proactively seeking their ideas and asking good questions.*

► *Seek the input and ideas of colleagues in decisions to find the best solution and to increase the chances for success.*

► *Be eager to learn, with an openness to new knowledge that will help the team provide consistently better care.*

► *Recognize the strength of our teaching programs in providing world-class care for patients today and preparing the next generation of tomorrow's professionals.*

► *Speak positively about colleagues and other departments, creating a higher degree of confidence and trust among patients and families.*

Partner with the community.

▶ *Appreciate that as Summit County's largest employer, Summa Health plays an important role in keeping our community strong, healthy and successful.*

▶ *Look for opportunities to give back to our community through volunteerism, which contributes to the health and vitality of the greater Akron region.*

▶ *Recognize that we serve diverse communities through our clinics, special programs and partnerships with other community agencies.*

What I love about this powerful document is that it is both inspiring (in statements like "Appreciate the privilege we have every day to serve our fellow man ...") and practical ("Make eye contact.") It has also been incredibly enduring; the statement was developed in 2017, and you can still find it on Summa's website today.

Among the six organizational characteristics that help prevent burnout, purpose is arguably the most foundational. A strong commitment to purpose helps moderate to some degree the impact the other five root causes of burnout can have on individuals and work teams. Better bosses help their team connect meaningfully and consistently to organizational purpose largely because they find strength in their own personal purpose as a leader. Their north-star values and sense of responsibility to the team help them find satisfaction and fulfillment in their role as a leader. Their strong sense of personal purpose supports and helps direct their individual team members in finding their own sense of purpose in their work.

CHAPTER 5

Why Better Bosses
Have to be Resilient

In the last chapter, I shared the outrage I heard from a senior executive to the widely held but simplistic view that helping people be more resilient was the answer to burnout during the pandemic. Given that I understand and largely share her opinion, it may be surprising that I've devoted this entire chapter to resilience. Relying too much on making frontline staff more resilient vs. recognizing that personal resilience helps leaders be more effective are two very different principles. Great bosses recognize and nurture their own personal resilience as a key part of their journey to becoming a more effective leader.

Resilience is among Dr. Linda Hill's eight qualities of exceptional leaders that I referenced in the Introduction to this book. While it is often overlooked when we think about traditional people-centric characteristics such as listening, respect, compassion, and empathy, resilience is absolutely crucial when the going gets tough for a team. And the reality is that the going does indeed get tough more often than not for leaders. Better bosses know that they need to be there for their team through thick and thin, so they focus on the development of their own personal resilience.

Bosses' level of resilience needs to develop and mature as they rise higher on the organizational ladder. One characteristic of well-functioning leadership hierarchies is that managers can lean on directors; directors can lean on vice presidents; and vice presidents can lean on the c-suite for support during difficult times. But who is the c-suite supposed to lean on? Often, the level above them — the Board of Directors — exerts more pressure than support during challenging financial or operational times.

Strong senior executives usually have found ways to successfully strengthen their personal resilience during their climb up the corporate ladder. This helps them to both effectively cope with the day-to-day stress they feel and to better support the people who work for them.

Better bosses begin to think about how they show up for their staff early in their careers. Am I helping to moderate the pressure and stress of difficult situations? Am I helping provide experienced counsel when my subordinates are struggling? Am I modeling measured, balanced responses to crises from the routine to the most chaotic? And am I providing a refuge of calm in the storm of day-to-day challenges that communicates in word and action, "We can get through this together?" The resilience exhibited by great bosses is the rock of stability that employees and other leaders need and look for in strong leaders.

Everyone's path to resilience is different. First, like other aspects of mental health, some individuals are just wired to be more resilient than others, either by nature or by nurture. Perhaps experiences in their childhood and young adult life have strengthened their coping mechanisms out of necessity because of the life cards they've been dealt. Life experiences also can cause setbacks at times, causing an individual to feel like they're losing ground in their ability to deal with challenges and be there for others in their personal and work lives.

But wherever you start, resilience doesn't get stronger without some level of focus and effort. The most resilient leaders I've worked for or with each paid attention to their own mental and physical health, which is the foundation of strong coping mechanisms.

In the Harvard Business Review article "5 characteristics of stress-resilient people (and how to develop them)", author Kandi Wiens, EdD, senior fellow at the University of Pennsylvania Graduate School of Education, describes insights from her research on leaders who flourish despite working in high-stress roles. [11] The five qualities and coping strategies she suggests align with my own personal experience, as well as what I've observed in successful leaders with a high degree of resilience.

1. They have a positive, optimistic outlook.
2. They have a problem-solving approach to stress.
3. They focus on what they can control.
4. They are adaptable and flexible.
5. They have strong relationships and social connections.

All these strategies have one critical element in common: they all recommend that you lean into the challenge to lessen the stress, not back away from it. In the classic response dichotomy described by psychologists, great leaders choose "fight" more often than they choose "flight." Theoretically, that makes sense. But in day-to-day practice, the challenge is not in understanding why resiliently leaning into stress and problems makes sense; the challenge is in sticking to the guidance when you are in the middle of a meltdown.

Withdrawing from stressful situations is not without merit or reason. Psychologists, counselors, and even pastors often recommend that when you have people or situations in your life that are pulling you down, increasing your stress, and/or generally making you unhappy, you need to disengage. While this may be a sound survival tactic for personal issues, it is a terrible strategy for bosses. Leaders who adopt this coping strategy to survive—either intentionally or instinctively—end up being described by their teams as distant, unavailable, out-of-touch, and unsupportive. This is a classic path to a very good, caring person becoming a bad boss.

Seeking and nurturing relationships with knowledgeable colleagues who will be respectfully honest with you will help you resist the temptation to back away. These social connections not only help you put life into perspective; the insights of someone who has the experience and perspective to understand what you're going through can help you identify blind spots and critically, rationally evaluate options.

While developing these relationships with peers and superiors within your organization is beneficial, it also is wise to find at least one trusted mentor outside your organization. What if your current daunting situation is with your boss, the CEO, or the Board of Directors of your company? Being too transparent and unguarded can come back to bite you, eventually making a tough situation even worse.

At the opposite end of the spectrum, great bosses come to understand the strength they can draw from their own team. When I was a CEO, I was constantly encouraged — and humbled — by how much staff appreciated my personal contributions and sacrifices. But that only happened because they felt like they knew me as a *person*, not just as a boss. I hear the same appreciation expressed by the frontline staff I work with in organizations today. Many see and readily admit that their manager has an impossible job, especially given the current workforce and financial pressures they are up against every day. Yes, staff want to be appreciated and recognized. But in highly functioning teams led by a great boss, they want to be supportive, too.

Major change that forever alters the direction and position of an organization does not happen without the risks associated with innovation and progress. Despite all the support I felt from the staff at Phoenix Children's Hospital when I was CEO, unexpected problems we encountered soon after building and opening the new campus, which was the first comprehensive, freestanding children's hospital in Arizona, inflicted a level of personal stress unlike any I'd ever experienced. A micro-burst storm that hit Phoenix only seven weeks after we opened the new hospital caused a clogged roof drain to break, pouring muddy rain water into the hallway outside of our operating rooms. The significant damage closed our surgery program for six weeks, which devastated our revenue budget at a time when we could least afford this type of crisis. For those who understand financial metrics, you'll appreciate just how serious the impact was; at one point we got down to 15 days cash-on-hand.

At about the same time, one of the most beloved physicians on our medical staff was in a devastating car accident that left him in a coma for over a week. Dr. Michael Teodori was not only an immensely talented pediatric cardiovascular surgeon; he was also a generous, supportive friend to me personally. While Mike miraculously recovered and eventually returned to practice, after the accident we all knew that his survival was far from assured given the severity of his injuries.

I tell this story because even someone who prides themselves on a high degree of personal resilience can be affected by unexpected, overwhelming life experiences. Strong, resilient leaders need to listen closely both to those who care about them — and to their own inner voice that's telling them they need help. Hopefully, increased openness and less shame around mental health in our society is reaching the executive offices of companies. Individuals know how excessive stress affects their overall health and well-being. But for leaders, the pressure to stay strong and just push through can be unyielding. I found myself struggling to focus; I was only getting a couple hours sleep each night, and I worried I was letting everyone down.

Even though my inner voice was telling me there was a problem, I refused to listen until two people who really cared about me — my wife and the hospital medical staff president — told me in no uncertain terms, "You need to take care of yourself and get some help." I did. And it made a remarkable difference at one of the most difficult, vulnerable times of my life. I remember that when I went to see my primary care physician, his nurse practitioner gave me the standard, 10-question survey that helps diagnose how anxiety and stress are affecting an individual. After completing the short questionnaire, all she needed to do was hand the survey back to me and calmly, compassionately say, "Look at how you answered these questions."

Smart bosses know that taking care of themselves and building their own personal resilience is essential to their success. But beyond personal well-being, it's also a critical factor in their organization's resilience during increasingly challenging times.

CHAPTER 6

Better Bosses
Understand the Power
in Empowerment

O f the six root causes of burnout, robbing employees of any voice or control of their day-to-day work is one of the least recognized but most influential factors affecting engagement and personal fulfillment.

In a 2021 study published in the journal Psychological Bulletin, the article title says it all: "Paths to the light and dark sides of human nature: A meta-analytic review of the prosocial benefits of autonomy and the antisocial costs of control." [12] The message is clear: when human beings have some say in how the work gets done, they feel valued, motivated, and engaged. When they don't, they feel like another cog in a giant machine where leaders don't care what they have to say.

Why do bosses who value and encourage autonomy have the most effective leadership style? The answer lies in their ability to help people find their own *intrinsic motivation*, not in anything they do to manage and motivate their actions directly. Then they empower team members with that intrinsic motivation to decide how best to achieve organizational, team, and personal goals to achieve the most significant and sustainable results.

Autonomy is powerful not only because it affects how people think about their work as individuals. It can powerfully impact how people frame their work in relation to their co-workers and the entire organization. The lead author explained the findings of his team's research in this way: "We found that consistently connecting people to the 'why' of their actions, providing choice in how tasks get done, and giving meaningful feedback results in people being more likely to share ideas and to be more collegial," emphasized James Donald of the University of Sydney Business School. "Managing with controlling, carrot-and-stick strategies led to people being less likely to share, cooperate, or to help others."

This insight points to another important aspect of the six root causes of burnout: they are all interrelated. In this case, a lack of empowerment inhibits employees' connection to purpose because they've stopped thinking about how their own actions and contributions help fulfill the organization's mission and values. Similarly, a lack of voice affects teamwork and the sense of community. When individuals' thoughts and ideas aren't encouraged, recognized, or appreciated, that impacts how open and cooperative they are with their colleagues, not just their boss.

When I think about a boss's role in staff empowerment, I remember one of those clever inspirational quotes that appear on motivational posters or LinkedIn posts: "When leaders stop listening, employees stop talking." But I've seen the impact of limited voice and empowerment be much more problematic and destructive than that; when bosses stop asking employees to share their best ideas and input, they stop thinking.

Why do bosses minimize employee voice?

When considering why bosses ignore their teams' ideas and suggestions, it is easy to write the problem off to an old-school "I'm the boss and you'll do what I say" mentality. In actuality, the issue is rarely that straightforward, unenlightened, or malicious. In my experience, it is unusual for bosses to really believe that they are so much smarter than their staff, or that they have nothing important or useful to contribute to improving the work environment, service to customers, or achievement of organizational goals.

Rather, our reluctance to give employees more voice is wrapped up in our own maturation as a leader. While empowering employees by giving them more voice in decision making may sound noble, the control that we're conceding has to come from somewhere. By giving employees more voice, we're giving up some degree of personal control. And that can be scary — even risky — especially when we're a new manager.

Hesitance to share control is largely due to an imperfect, immature, constrained view of our role as a leader, which creates blind spots of vulnerability related to employee voice. These faults tend to fall into two major categories: 1) challenges in our own transition to leadership, and 2) our organization's emphasis on reducing variability in our work.

Struggles transitioning from individual performer to a mentor of other people

Moving from star individual performer to manager is one of the most daunting leaps all of us make during our careers. And most of us have absolutely no idea how challenging — and risky — it will be. When we get that first big promotion to a leadership role, we only see the upside. All our hard work has been noticed and rewarded with a shiny new title and bump in pay. What's not to love?

Then reality sets in. We start to realize that the role of a middle manager is going to be much tougher than we thought.

As we're trying to adjust to the trials of having people who yesterday were our friends and peers report to us, we're also adjusting to increased pressure from above to deliver on operational, quality, and financial metrics. We're testing our new team to help us meet these goals, and they're testing us to see how supportive we'll be as their boss.

There's also an interesting dynamic that managers seldom admit but that can influence how we view our team, especially when staff seem to be pushing back against our new authority. The people reporting to us now are the same individuals who *didn't* get promoted when they were recruiting for the new leader role. Our perception — and to some extent the truth — is that they aren't as good as we are. Everyone has strengths, but the organization decided that it's our work performance, ability to get along with other people, business insights, and/or exceptional service to customers that was superior. Given that reality, it should not be surprising that new managers feel some degree of reluctance to cede control to individuals on their team.

This shift from star individual performer to essentially work choreographer is not unlike the actor's move from center stage to behind-the-scenes director. The star is in the spotlight with all eyes on them. They relish the applause just like frontline workers crave the appreciation and sense of satisfaction they get from serving customers. Like the director, a manager's sense of approval and fulfillment feels different; from backstage, they are often the unrecognized hero who holds things together for the team in good times and in bad.

In one study, doctors in Norway and the United Kingdom saw their managerial roles as "marginal" and lacking "gratification" compared to their past ones on the frontline. Given that as a manager we often experience more stress with less personal satisfaction, we shouldn't be surprised that we instinctively want to hold onto things that are important to us.

Higher engagement vs. more predictable, standardized processes

For all companies, consistently higher quality, delivered at lower costs, that exceeds customer expectations, is the holy grail of business and leadership. In the 1980s, leaders in many organizations were convinced that they had found the secret formula to achieving consistently better results in Lean and Six Sigma manufacturing methodologies. While the two philosophies are often uttered in the same breath, they originate from related but different motivations. Lean seeks to eliminate waste in processes, while Six Sigma works to reduce defects, conceptually to zero. In both methodologies, a foundational goal is to reduce variation, which causes waste and defects, and undermines quality.

The problem with contemporary process improvement philosophies and their focus on reducing variation is that they can breed a mentality of "we do it only this way." Period.

Of course, another foundational tenet of enlightened performance improvement methodologies is that the best solutions emerge when you involve the people in the trenches who are closest to the work. For Lean devotees, that's described as going to "Gemba," the place where value is created.

For frontline leaders in organizations that embrace Lean or Six Sigma-like structure and philosophies, the day-to-day practice of giving employees a voice can feel a bit schizophrenic. Does empowerment only live in the performance improvement box we create with PI committees and Kaizen events? When we're not in that box, having employees do what they've been told by following policies and procedures seems like the way we limit variation, which theoretically improves quality.

Smart bosses find ways to balance the benefits of standardization with the critical need to give employees some degree of voice and control. That can be in finding and encouraging smaller, team-based PI projects that give staff an opportunity to think about how the work might be done better or more efficiently, benefiting both employees and the customers they serve.

One of the best, most memorable examples of this philosophy I've seen was adopted by the Surgical Services team at Summa

Akron City Hospital. Playing on the advice, "How do you eat an elephant? One bite at a time," staff created a giant graphic of an elephant and hung it on the wall of the main hallway running through the heart of the department. Staff began to fill the elephant with puzzle-like pieces describing the small PI projects they tackled to solve digestible problems the team encountered. The beauty and genius in the approach went well beyond the process issues they solved; it was a visible reminder in the department that team members did indeed have a voice. They just needed to speak up.

In addition to being conscious of ways to give employees a voice, better bosses also pay attention to ways they may be taking it away inadvertently. For example, an underlying drive to reduce variation produced the idea that scripting employees was the best way to deliver consistent, predictably higher customer satisfaction and experience. The most common example is the familiar "it's my pleasure," phrase often heard at Chick-fil-A restaurants and Ritz-Carlton hotels. Yes, asking employees to repeat the three simple words it's, my, and pleasure seems relatively benign, but in a small way it takes away an employee's choice to respond to customers in a more personal manner that feels authentic, sincere and real to them. As an observer of human behavior in workplaces, including Chick-fil-A and the Ritz-Carlton, I've found that the a rote phrase "it's my pleasure" can be fine, but more meaningful expressions of customer service that connect to me as a person come from the heart, not the head.

My theory was confirmed and reinforced during a recent visit to my local Chick-fil-A. During a drive-through pick up, I realized that I hadn't paid attention to all of the detailed instructions in their upgraded mobile app. A QR code popped up, and I was supposed to stop and scan it near the beginning of the long drive-through "chute" that's characteristic of most of their restaurants. By the time I realized my mistake, I was past the point of no return. When I pulled up to the efficiently staffed pick-up window, I was ready to admit my mistake and volunteer to drive through again. I was shocked when the employee handed me my order, explaining that I had my iPhone location setting turned on in the Chick-fil-A app, so they knew when I pulled into their parking lot.

"Wow, that is damn impressive," I smiled. "Thank you for covering my screw-up and having my order ready." His reply was the crowning touch of the whole unexpected experience.

"Hey, man, we got your back. Enjoy your meal, OK?" were his parting words. I was so glad — and pleasantly surprised — that he didn't send me away with the plastic, "It's my pleasure."

The experience spoke volumes to me about that employee's boss, who behind the scenes was nurturing a work culture that reinforced, "You know how important customer satisfaction and loyalty are to us. I trust you to deliver it in the way that you think is going to be most effective ... in your own *voice*."

CHAPTER 7

Why Fairness is Fundamental to Being a Better Boss

A mong the six root causes of burnout identified by Dr. Christina Maslach, fairness is arguably the most subjective. Yes, it is important for bosses to recognize that being perceived as unfair can contribute to individual employees' disengagement and eventually burnout. But the challenge is that fairness is in the eyes of the beholder. What's viewed as reasonable and fair by one person may seem arbitrary and discriminatory to another.

"Life isn't always fair" is an outlook I adopted early in life. That response to life's challenges has served me well to avoid becoming embittered and obsessed with things I didn't like but couldn't change. The problem is the "life isn't fair; get over it" mindset is one that works well personally to deal with adversity, but it doesn't work for bosses. That attitude — even when it is meant to help individuals learn to cope with the fact that not everything is going to go their way — comes across as dismissive, uncaring, and unsympathetic.

Alternatively, trying to make everything fair for every member of your team doesn't work either. Smart bosses recognize that they can't make everything right in the world, their company, or even their own work group. Bosses who try too hard to make everything seem fair inevitably fail. While they may get credit from some for good intentions, most will see these efforts as futile and ungrounded.

Bosses who focus too much on making things fair for one or a few individuals risk losing credibility with the rest of the team. Relatively early in my career, I had a group of professionals working for me whose hours extended into the evening. Most other staff members in this wing of the building ended their day at around 5:00. The offices were securely locked, and there were other employees not too far away on the campus.

Despite these safeguards, one individual among a team of 15 employees in the department said that it wasn't fair that members of their team had to work alone in this area after hours. In response to her concerns regarding safety, we redoubled efforts to be sure entry points were secure and even installed a "panic button" that would immediately alert security officers onsite of a problem.

Unfortunately, these efforts were not enough. In a private meeting with me, she said, "I won't feel safe or satisfied until you post a dedicated security officer in the space with me." It was all I could do to keep my jaw from dropping to the floor. Logistically and financially, there was no way that we could accommodate this request, but I was still uber-focused on how to be fair to this employee and address her concerns.

For advice, I turned to one of the best HR directors I've ever worked with. Marlene listened to my story and reassured me that I had been more than fair in listening and trying to respond to this employee's concerns. Then she asked me a key question that I had completely ignored up to this point: "How is this affecting the other 14 employees in the department, and how do they feel about working in this area in the evening?"

It was like a huge lightbulb appeared above my head, and I saw the entire situation in a completely different — and much more balanced — way. The one disgruntled employee's demands were causing increasing frustration among the rest of the team. She complained to them on every shift and tried to coopt them into exerting more pressure on me to close this phone service for parents after hours, move them to a different location (which wasn't available), or hire the dedicated security officer for one person.

That conversation with Marlene gave me the path and resolve I needed to respectfully explain to this employee that we weren't going to do any of these things. But more than that, the experience taught me three things about how to think about fairness as a leader. Great bosses ask themselves three straightforward questions to assess whether or not they are being appropriately fair in any situation:

- ► *Have I listened to concerns openly and non-judgmentally?*

- ► *Am I treating all members of the team equitably?*

- ► *Have I thought through and clearly explained the rationale behind a decision, especially when it may be unpopular among some members of the team?*

Great bosses go beyond just thinking about these three questions when they are worried that a decision might be considered unfair. Here's how they incorporate the underlying philosophy behind the questions in their interactions with their teams every day.

Fairness starts with listening

The seeds of the perception of unfairness are sown when employees feel like they haven't been heard or that their boss doesn't fully understand their concerns. Better bosses learn to listen without bias, not only to communicate that they care but also to make sure they understand all sides of an issue. Assessing both the facts and the feelings around a problem helps bosses craft the most effective response to employees' issues when explaining a decision.

In many cases, bosses really do understand an issue much better than their staff give them credit for. In these cases, our natural inclination is to explain just how well we do get it, with facts and details that support our knowledge of the problem. Unfortunately, explaining often feels more like defending..

Even when we do fully understand, employees need to tell their story. How they tell that story provides insights for leaders on just how strongly they feel about a particular issue as well as the reasons behind the emotions. This helps us make the best final decision and how it will be implemented, which takes into consideration both the objective issues and subjective perceptions across the team.

Fair = equitable

In my work with frontline staff in a variety of organizations, I've heard over and over that staff assess whether their boss is fair on one thing: their willingness and ability to hold all members of the team equitably accountable for their work. High-performing employees don't find it unfair when they are sometimes called on to do more because of their expertise and experience. What they do find unfair is extra work that happens because others are not pulling their weight. It stings when there are no visible consequences for under-performers, and stars' extra efforts go unrecognized and seemingly unappreciated.

Holding all staff equitably accountable is one of leaders' most challenging jobs, especially early in their supervisory careers. It is also among the most important responsibilities they assume because of its impact on productivity, customer service, and quality. Additionally, it has an extraordinary impact on teamwork. Staff believe it is fair when all members of the team are held to a common, reasonable standard of performance. When that performance falls outside of the standard, better bosses provide feedback: positive for going above-and-beyond the standard, and negative when work falls short of expectations.

While this philosophy and practice make perfect sense in-tellectually, strong leaders also realize that consistently lower performers may feel like — and complain — that they are being "picked on." As long as you are holding staff equitably account-able to clearly communicated expectations, that's alright. The reality is that when you make too many exceptions, someone is going to feel like they are being treated unfairly. It is far better for lower performers to feel "singled out" than for high performers to believe that they are undervalued or exploited.

In some ways, holding staff equitably accountable has gotten more complicated with labor market and workforce changes. Staffing shortages in many industries are very real and impact a company's ability to provide products and services to meet market demand and community needs. Unless a lower performer violates a clear, black-and-white policy (like excessive absences or theft of property), their below-standard work falls into a gray area. Bosses who need to keep their department adequately staffed to meet demand and revenue targets are sometimes reluctant to offer constructive criticism because of the fear that people will leave. The theory is that a warm body is better than no body to keep staffing levels appropriate.

But that theory is short-sighted and the fear largely exaggerated. When constructive criticism is delivered in a straightforward, respectful way, there is scant evidence that average performers will resign. If they do, they were likely dragging down other members of the team and either weren't interested in or capable of getting better.

Another issue related to holding staff members equitably accountable may be even more sensitive and thus problematic in some people's eyes. But in terms of the contemporary challenges facing today's frontline leaders, I think it is important to put it on the table.

I was an early advocate for paying attention to diversity, equity, and inclusion in our workforce long before DEI was a well-recognized philosophy and strategy. I recognize value in a team of people with differing points of view born from their varying education, gender, racial and ethnic backgrounds, and ages. But I learned that respecting and paying attention to these factors shouldn't take precedence over an individual's skills, attitudes, and overall ability to do the best job for customers, the company, and their co-workers.

Many years ago, I had a wonderful person working for me who had been in the same position in the company for many years. In retrospect, she had grown more frustrated in her job than I let myself see. That frustration meant that her effectiveness as a boss had declined, and it was affecting the morale and engagement of her entire team.

She also was the only Black woman in a director role in the organization at the time.

Reflecting back, I realize now that I was more concerned with the fact that she represented sorely lacking diversity in the company than I was with her performance and my responsibility to provide fair, equitable feedback in areas where she needed to improve. My well-intentioned but misdirected priorities meant that she was unhappy and her staff were unhappy and less engaged as a result.

Ironically, a reorganization in the company meant that there would be a happy ending to this story. Her role was eliminated, but there was a new role in a completely different area that aligned with her interests and passions in the back half of her career. She flourished in the role, making important contributions to the company in a totally different way.

Better bosses understand the benefits and fairness of a diverse, inclusive work environment. But they don't sacrifice performance or leave individuals in roles where they are not fulfilled or successful to achieve it.

Explaining the "why" helps employees see the fairness in decisions

For most bosses on most days, it feels like you just can't win. Rarely are even the most straightforward decisions universally popular, and the critics often are more vocal in expressing displeasure than the supporters are in sharing praise. To maintain the peace, it is easy for bosses to fall into the decision-making trap that prioritizes less conflict over the right long-term direction for the team and company. Avoiding conflict today can compromise not only the best operational decisions; it potentially lays the foundation for additional problems down the road that can weaken relationships with employees and affect your perceived effectiveness as a boss.

That's why better bosses contemplate and then transparently communicate the "why" in actions and decisions that will have a material impact on their teams. Many well-intentioned bosses wait to explain the rationale behind a decision until after it is made and implementation begins. But that puts the emphasis on how to best "spin" a new plan or policy that they fear may not be well-accepted.

Better bosses embrace the advice of best-selling author Simon Sinek in his book, *Start with Why*. Sinek points out that when decision-making is not well-grounded in organizational and personal purpose, the "why" can be perceived as manipulative and dismissive of underlying concerns that have a significant impact on employees' day-to-day work and level of engagement.

When a bosses' decision processes have honestly, transparently considered the "why" at all stages of deliberation, they feel better equipped and more confident in communicating strategic and operational choices that are made to improve financial and operational performance. Even when decisions impact the team negatively in some ways, employees understand why they were made.

Using the acronym F.A.I.R. (Frame, Acknowledge, Instruct, and Respond) helps leaders remember the key factors they need to consider to explain and deploy decisions fairly.

Frame the context of the change

When employees are more aware of all the factors that have gone into a decision, there is a higher probability that they will see the changes as fair, even when aspects of the change affect them negatively. For example, a restaurant owner may be faced with the tough decision to end lunch service because the midday crowd continues to dwindle as more people work from home. Giving staff an idea of how much the lunch business has dropped and how that affects operating costs helps frame why the decision to focus only on dinner makes sense. In instances where communication has been transparent throughout an assessment or change process, the framing step becomes a reminder and affirmation of this open communication.

Smart bosses also recognize when not all factors related to a difficult decision can or should be shared openly during the process. For example, when a company is facing increasing financial pressures that threaten short- and long-term viability, I've never seen announcing that layoffs may be coming as a good idea — unless you actually want to encourage panic across the workforce that encourages your best employees to start looking for a new job now. In cases like layoffs or other human resources policies, framing is crucially important when the decision is announced to help individual employees process the personal impact it will have on them.

Framing is meant to help employees put the actions and decisions into a broader context, not to make them feel wonderful about a change that will have a negative impact on their lives and their work. That's why the next step is so important in improving acceptance and helping staff move on successfully.

Acknowledge the impact on people

Not all decisions can be beneficial to every person on your team. (On the rare occasions when they are, relish it!) Better bosses pay attention to how a process or policy change will affect their team members individually, then they candidly, openly acknowledge the inconvenience, dissatisfaction — even pain — that a decision may cause.

Old-school management theory discouraged leaders from being too apologetic regarding unpopular decisions for fear of looking weak or indecisive. The reality is that ignoring the real impact changes have on people's lives — whether innocently, inadvertently, or intentionally — makes leaders look out-of-touch, clueless, and unconcerned about employees' well-being and work satisfaction. The detachment doesn't make bosses look stronger. Rather, it creates more barriers to open, constructive communication that supports a more productive work environment.

That said, bosses also can go too far in leaning into empathy that turns into exaggerated sympathy. Bosses that either directly or indirectly communicate messages like, "This really is terrible, isn't it?" "You guys are being treated unfairly" or "I'm not sure how we'll cope with this change" are often reflecting their own personal frustrations, not truly trying to understand the emotions and struggles of the team. Empathy is beneficial; pity is paralyzing and disheartening.

I discovered the power in sincerely acknowledging the unfair impact difficult decisions can have on employees while I was CEO at Phoenix Children's Hospital. I shared earlier the struggles we encountered because of a micro-burst rainstorm that flooded our operating rooms. One of the toughest decisions we had to make that year was suspending pay increases for our hard-working team. We framed the decision in terms of all the devastating things that had happened to us and the financial impact it had on our budget. More importantly, we acknowledged the impact that the decision had on our people. I remember exactly what I said to staff in the town hall meetings we held during that time.

"I realize that all of you have worked harder than you've probably ever worked in your lives to open this beautiful new hospital for the children and families in Arizona. Now that we're open, we've had to make the difficult decision not to give you a pay raise this year. And that really sucks. I'll be eternally grateful for all the sacrifices you've made over the past couple of years. I thank you, but more importantly, the families in our community thank you. They know what a difference you make for their kids."

Impart knowledge and support

When organizations change course, implement new policies, or make tough decisions, great bosses are there alongside their teams to provide support and guidance during implementation. High visibility during times of change and challenge are essential for two major reasons.

First, staff need to know that their boss really understands the impact — both positive and negative — that the change is having on the team. That happens through direct observation and during open, honest, unfiltered conversations about how things are going. Leadership visibility is always important to keep bosses connected and aware of what's really happening on the frontlines. During times of change and challenge, presence is essential to maintain staff morale and engagement.

Second, bosses are in leadership roles for a reason. Their progression up the leadership ladder in a company has happened because they bring specific technical or operational expertise, possess the ability to effectively solve problems in a collaborative way, and build strong working relationships with colleagues. All of these skills can be extremely helpful to a team when they are navigating new or rough waters.

React to resolve issues

Great bosses empower their teams to step up and play a role in solving their own problems. That doesn't mean that they stand by at a distance when staff are struggling with challenges their boss could help them overcome. Like in any strong, enduring partnership, better bosses are there for their teams in good times to celebrate achievements and collectively bask in the glow of success. But it's the bad times that test the strength of a partnership and allow it to grow. How leaders show up during challenging times significantly impacts how teams judge their sense of fairness.

CHAPTER 8

Great Bosses Build Great Teams

U p to this point, we've focused on how bosses build trust, confidence, and engagement with individual team members. While those relationships are foundational to leadership success, better bosses understand and care about more than just their personal connection with staff. They also recognize the importance of the relationships that team members have with each other.

Thinking back to the root causes of burnout, remember that the lack of a strong, supportive *community* in the workplace is one of the contributing factors to employee frustration and disengagement. When colleagues don't get along and can't count on one other, especially during challenging times, workforce morale and overall well-being suffer, which diminishes productivity and operating results.

A simplistic view of what constitutes a strong work community has everyone getting along, becoming friends, and all thinking alike. But that view is unrealistic. Today's workforce is as diverse as it has ever been. Long gone are the days when "community" meant that everyone looked alike, dressed alike, and thought alike. Think of IBMers of the 1960s. You knew someone worked for IBM by their dark suit, crisply pressed white dress shirt, and conservative tie. But "uniform" applied to more than their outfit; it described the way IBMers thought, spoke, and approached their jobs.

CEO Thomas Watson Jr. believed adamantly in one of the company's core values: respect for the individual. However, that respect didn't include an appreciation of each individual employee's differing thoughts, ideas, and opinions. Rather, the cradle-to-grave employment ethos assured workers that IBM would not eliminate jobs regardless of ups-and-downs in the economy, business cycle, or profitability. IBM's definition of loyalty to the individual garnered intense reciprocal — and often blind — loyalty to the company by its employees.

Through the 1970s, IBM and its culture of market leadership and steadfast loyalty to employees was the envy of business leaders across the globe. The IBM philosophy and community based on loyalty and conformity worked extremely well. Until it didn't.

The company's dedication to the development, sales, and service of massive mainframe computers caused it to minimize and largely miss the emerging personal computer revolution. Revenue and market share dropped as the company's massive infrastructure and overhead became more oppressive, literally choking the life out of the enterprise. By the early 1990s, IBM was running out of cash and desperate for a major turnaround.

To save IBM, the Board of Directors hired the first CEO from outside the company, Louis Gerstner from RJR Nabisco. In an early speech, Gerstner was clear that IBM needed "a series of very tough-minded, market-driven strategies" that would increase shareholder value. Among those was a massive 60,000-person layoff, the first in the company's history.

Because of these dramatic moves, the company survived and returned to profitability. What didn't survive was IBM's uniform, paternalistic culture. If there had been a funeral for IBM's core culture and values, the body in the casket would have been wearing a dark blue suit and white dress shirt.

Most of the leadership lessons from IBM's decline and eventual turnaround cite two issues: 1) prioritizing loyalty to employees over shareholder value, and 2) becoming so obsessed with one product line that you miss major market and technological shifts. A less obvious but arguably more important lesson for bosses to understand is that less uniformity across the workforce requires different leadership skills and practices to create a strong sense of community and teamwork.

A 2024 article in Forbes, "One More Time: Why Diversity Leads to Better Team Performance," [13] delineates the benefits of a workforce where team members come from different places, different backgrounds, and different ideas:

- ► Increasing innovation and learning
- ► Creating a more inclusive and safe environment for people to speak their minds
- ► Retaining top talent
- ► Accelerating complex problem-solving with more perspectives and ideas
- ► Enhancing morale through greater sense of belonging

But while the organizational advantages of a diverse, inclusive workforce are well-documented, DEI as a national priority took a major hit with the second inauguration of Donald Trump as president in 2025. DEI programs were dismantled, defunded, and discredited in government agencies and those organizations receiving government funding. Many public and private corporations pulled back on their visible support of DEI as well.

The debate over the benefits and drawbacks of diversity programs in organizations will likely continue for many years without achieving consensus on one right path forward. For bosses in the trenches, perhaps companies have put too much emphasis on achieving an ill-defined appropriate level of diversity and not enough attention on *how* to lead a diverse work team effectively.

Whether you believe that DEI programs are absolutely essential or went too far, the reality is that our workforce today is more diverse in more ways than it has ever been. Gender, generational, racial, ethnic, economic, and ideological shifts over the past 50 years mean that the employee base in most companies looks nothing like the largely white male workforce at IBM in the 1960s. For bosses leading inherently diverse teams, focusing on how to make a work team more diverse distracts from a much more important challenge: how to make inclusion and belonging an enabler of higher performance and engagement.

The hard truth is that leading a diverse work team is more challenging than one that is homogeneous. Ensuring everyone has a voice while still making definitive, timely, appropriate decisions that may not be universally popular isn't easy. Let's explore the most important ways that great bosses overcome these challenges and develop teams that accomplish more — in better ways — together.

Make working well together a clearly articulated priority

Teams must know exactly where their boss stands on the importance of teamwork. That means better bosses unequivocally explain the importance they place on respecting each other's skills and contributions. Great leaders then support that stated philosophy with actions that seek out and lean into the unique strengths, experiences, and accomplishments of each team member to get things done efficiently and successfully.

Granted, words only get you so far. But strongly expressing your expectations around teamwork is an essential starting point. That declaration should be straightforward to be most powerful: "Teamwork is a non-negotiable for me. I expect you all to get along and respect one another, even when you may have different ideas and opinions."

Model what great teamwork looks and feels like

Better bosses set a high bar for themselves first when it comes to exemplifying the characteristics of great teamwork. Stating the importance of mutual support is important, but their actions speak much louder when their goal is to achieve high levels of cooperation and meet challenging goals. Simply what employees *see* is what we *get* as leaders related to teamwork.

Especially when the going gets tough, caring bosses show up and pitch in to help their team. But that doesn't mean that bosses are always stepping into individual staff members' jobs. The most effective managers understand that always being in the trenches doing the work of frontline staff can start to make them look like a martyr, not a strong leader. Employees appreciate their boss being available to step in where they are needed to run interference and solve problems on the fly. They can't do that when they are always covering a single staff member's role.

Respect for other team members is foundational to effective teamwork. For that reason, respect is the personal characteristic inspiring bosses model every day in their interactions with every employee. When providing constructive criticism to point out and correct a problem behavior, for example, they always respect the individual and their dignity, even though they dislike their behaviors or actions.

Embrace diverse experiences and expertise to improve performance

Everyone thinking alike, looking alike, and behaving alike can create a very comfortable, seemingly safe environment, whether it's in your community, church, civic organization, or place of work. It can also breed complacency and an unwillingness to challenge the status quo to improve service, quality, and operating results.

For enlightened bosses, their team's diverse backgrounds, experiences, and talents are a means to a critical end: better performance for customers, employees, and ultimately shareholders. They regularly lean into the differences across their team — individually and collectively — to surface new ways of thinking about old problems and challenges.

Smart bosses recognize and openly admit that a workplace culture where individuals come from different places with differing ideas inherently creates tension. That natural tension can be disruptive — even destructive — if it is not skillfully managed to create a sense of constructive questioning and a will to always make things better.

When I personally think back about decisions that were in some ways flawed, I have to humbly admit that there were usually people on the team who had concerns about the direction we were going. I realize now that naysayers can be extremely important. Rather than ignoring them and hoping they eventually go away, wise bosses ask them to explain their concerns, being smart about whether to solicit their feedback publicly in team meetings or privately in one-on-one conversations. Sometimes being more open to hearing and understanding what can feel like negative grumbling helps us make better, less risky decisions.

That said, no decision is perfect. Doing nothing or indefinitely delaying a decision may feel safe in the short term, but inaction is extremely dangerous in the long term. What discerning bosses don't do is allow their teams to become permanently paralyzed because they can't reach consensus on every decision.

Counsel — or sacrifice — strong performers who create more dysfunction than constructive conversations

A strong team embraces and thrives on different points of view and healthy debate. What they don't appreciate is a colleague who doesn't respect others.

Early in my career, I worked with one of the smartest, hardest working individuals I've ever met. This person had a huge scope of responsibility and was always anxious to take on more for the organization. But his exaggerated sense of duty was rooted in the fact that he didn't believe any other member of the team could do the job quite as well. At heart, it came down to a lack of respect for the skills, experience, and opinions of his colleagues.

Of course, other members of the team quickly sensed and were offended by this absence of respect. The dynamics within the team went from discomfort to dysfunction, which ultimately affected the success of the division and the organization.

Gifted bosses watch for and are willing to address a work environment where diverse thought deteriorates into dysfunction. Counseling the individual who has become an island within the team should always be the first step. But when that doesn't change behaviors, wise bosses recognize that the performance of a strong, diverse team always exceeds the strong performance of a single individual, regardless of how smart and hard working that individual may be.

Helping people work better together is one of the most important and powerful skills of great bosses. It also is one of the most nuanced and challenging competencies to develop and leverage, especially when working with a diverse team of strong individual performers.

CHAPTER 9

The Underappreciated Potential in Purpose

What's my purpose in life? It's a question man has been asking for centuries, with roots in both philosophy and psychology. Over the past decade, contemplating purpose has become a priority for more than just reflective individuals; it has become an important question for companies.

Thinking about purpose helps leaders frame and better ground decisions ranging from high-level strategic direction to tactical priorities in customer service. Having a powerful sense of purpose provides context for the things a company and its people do every day. But the benefits of understanding purpose go far beyond just strategic and operational clarity. Perhaps the greatest benefit of affirming a company's purpose is the impact it can have on its workforce.

Why we exist is a powerful question not just for companies but also for the people who work in those companies. Workers who understand their personal purpose and the importance of their roles are more engaged, fulfilled, and committed to their work. This connection to something bigger than themselves and the paycheck they get each week helps them through the day-to-day frustrations and setbacks that are bound to occur in any organization. Employees who find purpose in their work benefit from a steadfast foundation of core principles that positively influence everything they do, much the way their faith, closest personal relationships, or non-religious spirituality influence their personal lives.

Great bosses understand that to help their staff develop and strengthen their sense of purpose in work, they must find their own connection to purpose in leadership. But that can be more challenging than it sounds on the surface.

Let's be honest: being a boss can be a thankless job. In our work with frontline staff, we've found that most employees recognize their boss's job is often impossible. When rationalizing why bosses put up with additional work, stress, and problems, employees often explain it away with a version of, "Well, that's why they pay them the big bucks."

But in many industries and organizations, the bigger bucks hardly seem adequate compensation for the additional burdens that bosses bear. When companies are under pressure to reduce costs, increase volume and revenue, and/or improve quality, the onus of delivering on these company-wide imperatives usually falls primarily to middle managers. Staffing shortages and frontline employees' changing attitudes toward work in general further complicate expectations for managers to achieve better results.

Historically, more than just money has driven high-performing, competitive individuals to pursue supervisory positions. Moving into management is often seen as the only way to advance a career and gain higher visibility and status in the company. Becoming "the boss" presumably means more say and control over both individual responsibilities and direct reports. But especially in large organizations, new leaders frequently end up feeling disappointed and disillusioned.

In the Harvard Business Review article, "Research: Becoming a Manager Doesn't Always Feel Like a Step Up," authors Nishani Bourmault and Michael Anteby looked at why employees moving up to management experienced what they described as "managerial blues." [14] In one study, they found drivers in the Paris subway system who were promoted to managers often experienced unexpected disappointment in their new roles. They explained that in their old frontline jobs they dealt with life-and-death situations, feeling a great degree of responsibility for and connection to the lives of others.

"On one subway train, there are approximately 600 to 800 passengers," one driver explained, "so we are responsible for all of the passengers, for their safety, for everything that happens." While new managers reported some positive aspects of their new roles, many did not find them as meaningful as being a driver. "Really, we do nothing that matters," one manager admitted.

To avoid this demoralizing disappointment, better bosses learn to cultivate and embrace a new type of purpose that's centered on supporting, mentoring, and developing other people. Like proud parents internalize and celebrate the successes of their children, great managers share a sense of accomplishment and fulfillment when members of their team succeed. They publicly acknowledge and praise their employees' achievements, while privately savoring a sense of personal satisfaction in the role they played in individuals' or the team's success.

For both new and seasoned bosses, finding this sense of pride and joy in the accomplishments of others doesn't usually happen automatically or by accident. Certain intentional leadership practices that connect you more meaningfully to the work of your team will help you connect to your personal purpose as a boss.

Stay connected to your team and your customers

Some believe that leadership visibility at the frontline — whether you call it "going to gemba" or "management by walking around" — is all about supporting staff and customers. But when done well and in the right spirit, bosses can draw just as much fulfillment from the experience as the staff they're engaged with. Staying connected with your team in the trenches where the real work happens builds a level of trust and openness. That connection makes it comfortable for staff to tell you honestly what's going on and what needs to improve. As your relationship develops and deepens, employees also find it easier to tell you — occasionally — how much they notice and appreciate what you do as their boss.

As a boss, I think the gratitude my staff expressed for the work I was doing meant more to me than praise coming from above. I still remember one day when I was rounding in our neonatal intensive care unit at Phoenix Children's Hospital. The NICU was a huge, high acuity, high stress environment that was staffed by some of our most talented, dedicated nurses. While the work could be extremely rewarding, I also knew it was a challenging place to work.

Making sure our staff felt heard and appreciated was especially important, so I probably pushed them a bit more intently to share any questions or issues that were on their minds. After my second or third insistence that I really did want to hear any concerns they had, one of the nurses looked at me directly and firmly said, "No, really, we don't have any questions for you right now, OK?"

With that message clearly received, I turned and started to walk away. As I did, I heard something from the same nurse that meant the world to me. "But Mr. Stamp, please don't stop walking around and asking us if we have any questions," she said. "It makes us feel good when you walk through the unit." That simple, heartfelt statement made me feel good, too. While I doubt that at the time I thought about the encounter in these terms, what I felt that day was a strong sense of purpose. The staff in the NICU made an incredible difference in the lives of the babies and families they were taking care of. And in that moment, I felt like I was making a meaningful difference, too.

Whether you are a new manager or the CEO, talking with customers can be incredibly rewarding — and humbling — as well. Especially when you're having a rough, discouraging day, finding a way to connect with your customers reminds you of what's really important and why you're there in the first place. Nine times out of ten, you'll hear about the amazing skill, service, compassion, and commitment of your team. And those first-hand comments will give you the opportunity to share with staff specific compliments about the difference they're making. Those expressions of gratitude make them feel good — and extending them will make you feel even better.

Conversations with unhappy customers are extremely important, as well. In addition to helping prioritize areas for improvement for the team going forward, having a customer yell at you for a problem in your organization helps you better understand what your employees hear and put up with every day. Staff members appreciate bosses who may not be able to do every part of their job, but who sincerely try to understand the challenges they are up against.

Think about and relish why supporting staff is an honorable, vitally important responsibility

Too often, organizations and new managers spend the majority of their time emphasizing the management, not the people-centric leadership, side of their role. While it is important to manage the budget, KPI reporting, and the staffing matrix, these necessary tasks will never be as rewarding as leading a dedicated team and helping them be at their very best. That's the job of a great, supportive boss. The budget and KPI reports will never tell you what a great job you did when you paid attention to them. But your team members will. When a strong, connected boss invests the time, empathy, and care to connect with their team in meaningful ways, their personal purpose as a leader becomes clear — and incredibly satisfying.

For bosses, discovering their own sense of meaning and purpose in leading others is essential but insufficient to instill that same sense of purpose in their employees. Leveraging purpose must be intentional, authentic, enduring, pervasive, and central to how work gets done in the organization. Let's examine some of the ways great bosses at all levels of a company can begin to make that happen.

Collaboratively explore your collective purpose

All companies have mission, vision, and values statements. These official proclamations highlight *what* we do (mission), *where* we're going (vision), and *how* we will behave getting there (values). A companion purpose statement speaks to *why* we exist as an organization. Aligned with the traditional mission, vision, and values, a purpose statement focuses on the meaning of work and the role of the organization in relation to all key constituencies: customers, families, staff and the larger community. For bosses, an inspiring, meaningful statement of organizational purpose can provide a solid foundation to help staff develop their own personal sense of purpose and meaning in their work.

A well-facilitated, collaborative design workshop over a couple of intense days is the most efficient, effective way to consider and construct a powerful purpose statement. Harnessing extant but untapped passion around the company's work, this streamlined design process brings together your "stars" from all levels of the organization — except the C-suite. I've found that these types of groups work best when people in the belly of the company — those who represent the very best of who you are and what your company represents — are empowered by senior executives to think about the importance of their work to customers, colleagues, and the community. While the C-suite still gets to review and ultimately approve the team's final draft, I've seldom seen them make any substantive changes because they are so impressed and inspired by the work.

That's exactly what happened when I worked with Hillsdale Hospital in south central Michigan. Located in a scenic, rural county of 47,000 people, Hillsdale is only about an hour from several major cities with large health care organizations, including Detroit, Ann Arbor, Toledo, and Kalamazoo.

So, how can a smaller organization like Hillsdale Hospital possibly compete against much larger, competitive health care systems? Much of the answer lies in understanding their purpose. Here's the compelling purpose statement that a small group of dedicated, exemplary employees developed through a focused, facilitated process like I described:

> *Hillsdale Hospital exists to ensure that our region has access to a full range of high quality health services close to home. Through the dedication of our talented staff and support of our generous community, we provide exceptional care to our neighbors.*

What a group of dedicated, loyal staff members came to better understand through this process was that their organization isn't just about providing health care services. They are a vital part of the small Hillsdale community, taking care of their families and friends. This passion and connection to purpose helped employees find their own personal purpose serving their community.

But even in companies that have thoughtfully developed and widely communicated an inspiring organizational purpose statement, words in those declarations are meaningless unless they make it all the way to the frontline and impact the way staff feel about their work. Bosses can't expect the connection to purpose to happen naturally, even in organizations with a naturally benevolent mission. Each employee has to internalize and embrace purpose for it to make a meaningful difference for them personally and for their company collectively. Strong bosses in the middle of the organization play a pivotal role in making that happen in the following ways.

Find meaning in the positive, not just problem-solving

Contemporary process improvement models such as LEAN and Six Sigma are built on diagnosing and fixing deficiencies and problems. For both workers and a company's customers, this continuous improvement mentality makes things better for everyone. But there is a potential downside, too. When a flaw-focused mindset permeates organizational culture, teams can miss and underappreciate all of the positive things they are accomplishing every day.

Appreciative inquiry, a model developed by the Department of Organizational Behavior at Case Western Reserve University in 1987, was the precursor of positive organization studies and the strengths-based movement in American management. [15] Among the model's five core principles, the "poetic" and "positive" principles are particularly important for building social capital and finding meaning in work:

- ▶ **Poetic Principle** — Organizational life is expressed in the stories people tell each other every day, and the story of the organization is constantly being re-authored.

- ▶ **Positive Principle** — Momentum and sustainable change requires positive affect and social bonding.

Leveraging the appreciative inquiry philosophy means rethinking and supplementing traditional organizational practices focused on improvement. And that starts with effective storytelling.

Learn how to tell — and encourage — great stories

As suggested in appreciative inquiry's poetic principle, stories are a compelling way to capture the essence of what's best in an organization. Much more than just reporting positive operating results, stories capture the richness of individual employees' contributions in a way that makes a company's stated values really come to life.

Great stories don't get to the point too quickly. They are not a dryly delivered report of the outcome of an encounter with a customer or colleague. Instead, they paint a visual — and often emotional — picture of exactly what happened and why it was so meaningful. Here's an example of a wonderful story told to me many years ago that I've repeated many times in workshops to illustrate the benefit of a strong workforce culture.

On a cold winter morning in St. Louis, about six inches of snow had fallen overnight and hadn't yet been cleared from the parking lots at Progress West Hospital. When John Antes, the hospital president, arrived at work at six a.m., he noticed a staff member cleaning off her car with a scraper in the bitter cold and decided it would be a nice thing to help her. (As an aside, the first time I heard this story, I thought the CEO stopping to clean snow off an employee's car was the inspirational endpoint.) As John approached the car, the ER nurse insisted that he didn't need to stop and help, but she soon realized that he had a scraper in hand and wasn't going to be deterred.

"So, how busy was the ER last night with all of the snow coming down?" John asked. The nurse sheepishly explained that she wasn't coming off the night shift but instead starting her shift soon. Perplexed, he asked, "So, why was your car here last night?"

The nurse smiled and admitted, "Well, actually, this isn't my car. I got here a little early this morning and noticed this car parked in a handicap space. I knew a family member was probably going to struggle to clear off their car when they came out this morning. I had some extra time, so I decided to clear it for them."

This example is powerful for several reasons. First, it is an incredibly good story. Just saying a kind nurse helped clean snow off a family's car just wouldn't have had the same impact. Second, it reinforces how much of the power in storytelling is in the retelling. This story spread like wildfire through the hospital, with hundreds of employees inspired to mirror this nurse's commitment to really living the organization's values. And, finally, it illustrates what a real sense of purpose looks and feels like. This nurse understood her purpose went well beyond just providing technical, clinical care in the emergency room.

Help employees connect their work to a bigger picture of what's really important

Bosses' jobs are tough, and so are the jobs of the people who work for them. Day-to-day hassles, bureaucratic red tape, and occasionally unreasonable customer expectations can easily bring down even the most positive, optimistic person. Great bosses don't gloss over the challenges their employees face. They also don't let them wallow in unproductive self-pity for too long. The best bosses acknowledge and work collaboratively to reduce hassles where possible, but they also help staff see a balanced, bigger picture that includes the importance and impact of the work they do every day.

For example, regulatory oversight is a reality in many industries. Regulators and inspectors are by role and by nature often nitpickers. They have a list of hundreds of isolated practices that they have the authority and sometimes exaggerated sense of personal responsibility to check for. Collectively, these practices help ensure safety and quality. But for hard working frontline staff, regulatory surveyors' reports can feel overly critical, discouraging, and overwhelming.

Great bosses help put things in perspective. They acknowledge the need to fix and improve, but they also remind the team of the big picture: the impact their work is having on customers' lives every day. That impact is framed not just in terms of overall quality and customer service metrics, but in meaningful stories.

Great bosses discover and nurture a strong sense of personal purpose in leading, supporting, and developing the people who work for them. They also help those individuals find their own path to purpose that contributes to their success, well-being, and fulfillment in their work.

PART TWO

CHAPTER 10

A Playbook to Become a Better Boss

I t is rare that I disagree with the premise or findings of a Harvard Business Review article. But when I saw the headline, "Don't Let Lazy Managers Drive Away Your Top Performers," [16] I was skeptical — and offended on behalf of all the hard-working bosses I know who are up against increasing pressure to effectively manage today's workforce challenges.

Then I read the first paragraph of the article:

> *"Many people believe that being a good manager only requires common sense, and that it is therefore easy to be one. If this were true, good managers would be commonplace at all levels of more organizations, and as a result, employee engagement and retention would be high. However, only 13% of workers*

worldwide are engaged at work, and employee turnover rates in the United States are at a 17-year high. As these statistics suggest, either most managers lack common sense, or good management is, in fact, quite challenging in practice."

Good management is, indeed, very challenging. In the organizations I've worked with, I seldom find bosses who are lazy. What I often do find are managers who feel ill-prepared to effectively engage and mentor the employees who work for them, especially given our constantly changing labor landscape. Even among experienced managers with a strong track record of success, I hear, "I need help. This is a totally different world than a few years ago. Things that worked earlier in my career as a leader just don't seem to be effective anymore. I need a new plan."

While the headline in the HBR article may have been exaggerated, most of the content accurately portrays the state of employee engagement and bosses' response in organizations. Two specific symptoms the authors cite certainly align with my in-the-trenches experience: 1) managers have a tendency to blame low performance and turnover on employees rather than on themselves or the organization, and 2) managers often look for quick fixes to complex retention problems.

To drive better employee engagement and operating results, bosses need a well-defined framework of evidence-based leadership competencies and practices. This leadership playbook provides the scaffolding around which great bosses build their own individualized approaches to team engagement and employee development. An evidence-based framework frees bosses from the burden of reinventing the wheel to improve staff engagement and development. It is the respectful answer to the cry of "help!"

I hear from frustrated managers coping with excessive turnover, high vacancy rates, and individual employee indifference.

A recent conversation I had with a friend who is a senior executive in a large organization illustrates why offering a more detailed playbook makes so much sense. Exasperated by current staffing and financial challenges, he admitted that their employee engagement, retention, and morale were at all-time lows. He also reluctantly confessed that for the first time in his career, he didn't see a clear path out of the current morass.

Looking for a bright spot, he quickly shared, "But managers are doing action plans coming off of our employee engagement survey to try to turn things around."

Since we were both being open and candid with one another, I asked, "Have you really found those action plans to be effective?"

Without hesitation, he admitted, "No, you're right. We usually check off the box that they're done, then they go on the shelf, and we don't look at them again."

The conventional fix to such a problem would be a structured documentation and reporting system that required managers to submit monthly reports on the status of all improvement tactics. In today's environment, where frontline leaders are stressed and stretched more than ever before, it is probably also a recipe for middle manager mutiny.

Below are three big reasons well-meaning action plans just don't work.

1.   Well-meaning bosses believe more creative means more effective

In well-meaning attempts to get staff more engaged, I've seen all kinds of creative solutions: staff lounge holiday decorating contests, bulletin boards featuring baby photos, and recognition/ rewards programs featuring prizes and trinkets. These are all fun ideas. But at the risk of sounding like a killjoy, these creative ideas miss the mark on what staff really want and need to feel connected, engaged, empowered, and fulfilled in their jobs.

2. Well-meaning bosses ask frontline staff, "What do you want me to do?"

Yes, giving staff more voice is a key element of successful leaders' engagement and retention strategy. But when a work team's culture lacks foundational elements of trust, inclusion, and transparency, employees are going to be reluctant to share what they really want — and need. If engagement and work team culture is poor, are team members really going to candidly tell their manager, "You don't listen to us," "You play favorites," or "You're never around when we really need you"?

3. Well-intentioned bosses simply aren't sure what to do

Frontline leaders themselves are feeling burned out and uncertain about how to rebuild work team engagement. If asked to create an action plan, conscientious leaders begrudgingly will develop something. But in their hearts, they often doubt that it will make a difference. And when the momentary glow from the breakroom decorating contest fades, turnover is still high and little has meaningfully improved — for the staff and their dedicated boss.

Rather than asking every manager to invent their own plan to improve engagement, smart organizations leverage the abundant research on evidence-based leadership practices proven to move the needle on staff morale, retention, and job fulfillment. The **T.E.A.M. Leadership Playbook**, which I developed over 10 years ago in my work with teams and their bosses, does just that. The T.E.A.M. framework offers a practical, straightforward launch pad for bosses to rethink not only what they're doing each day but *how* they're engaging their staff.

Teach
Team Huddles
Inclusive Staff Meetings
Integrated Rounding

Empower
Shared Decision-Making
Workgroup PI Projects

Align
Workgroup Goals
Reporting Results

Mentor
Frequent Feedback
Development Dialogues
Observation

my**TEAM**.®

T.E.A.M. trades discreet tasks for four overarching responsibilities that help a manager become a better boss: *teaching, empowering, aligning,* and *mentoring.* These leadership themes incorporate key insights and implications for bosses from Dr. Christina Maslach's research on burnout and the six root causes underlying symptoms of cynicism, depersonalization, and inefficacy.

Here's how the competencies and leadership practices of T.E.A.M. help bosses more effectively engage, lead, and develop staff.

TEACH: providing visible, consistent support for all employees as a collective team

Effective leaders are great teachers, and great teachers are always learning. As teachers, successful bosses offer the expertise and wisdom that shape the group's success. Of course, servant leaders also learn from the knowledge and insights of their front-line employees to make the team stronger.

At all levels, strong leaders are highly visible. They engage in meaningful conversations with both staff and customers, share real-time information that helps employees do their jobs better, and facilitate inclusive work group meetings that encourage dialogue and feedback.

EMPOWER: incorporating staff voice into day-to-day work and decisions affecting the team

At the heart of all contemporary performance improvement methodologies is the idea that better solutions emerge when you involve the people closest to the work. Large, complex projects often involve cross-functional groups drawn from many departments. However, strong bosses also look for focused departmental projects that include employees in decision-making and designing better ways to do things. They understand that employee voice is an essential part of the way the team functions day-to-day, permeating everything from major projects to routine problem-solving.

ALIGN: structuring and tracking goals that impact individuals' purpose and performance

Most organizations have become adept at setting well-defined, measurable goals at the corporate level. But to more effectively involve staff up-and-down the organization in the achievement of these broad goals, collaborative bosses help their teams set more tactical, leading goals at the frontline.

Establishing more specific, behavior-focused plans at the work group level is just the first step in using goals to effectively involve employees in improvement efforts. Consistently tracking, reporting, and discussing progress with the team helps strengthen the group's sense of purpose and resolve in achieving their goals.

MENTOR: shaping individuals' development through consistent, balanced feedback

Mentoring staff to improve individual and collective performance is arguably a manager's most important job. Too often, leaders associate feedback only with negative or constructive criticism. But to improve morale and build high-performance cultures, supportive bosses use positive feedback to reinforce success and reward great results. In addition to creating a culture of recognition and appreciation, balanced feedback helps employees more readily embrace constructive criticism. Feedback that only points out mistakes or short-comings is demoralizing and aggravates turnover, especially among top performers.

Using the T.E.A.M. framework, the following four chapters explore specific, evidence-based strategies that better bosses leverage to bring the model to life.

CHAPTER 11

TEACH:

Why Bosses Must Be Great Teachers—and Lifelong Learners

"I am a teacher. It's how I define myself. A good teacher isn't someone who gives answers out ... but is understanding of needs and challenges and gives tools to help other people succeed. That's the way I see myself. So whatever it is that I will do eventually after politics, it'll have a lot to do with teaching."

— JUSTIN TRUDEAU,
Former Prime Minister of Canada

E xceptional bosses are great teachers. And great teachers are inquisitive, constant learners.

Organizations seldom describe the role of an effective manager as "teacher." But indeed, the philosophy described by Canadian Prime Minister Trudeau captures the essence of what it means to lead a team in a way that nurtures staff engagement and maximizes results.

That's why the first and foundational component of the T.E.A.M. Model is "Teach."

Think about the traits of one of your best teachers. Certainly, they were knowledgeable. But it's doubtful that imparting facts and figures was the primary reason that they came to mind. Their ability to inspire, ignite curiosity, and create an environment where you could be at your very best were more likely the characteristics that made the biggest impact on you.

Of course, to be inspiring and motivating, managers first and foremost must be visible and appropriately engaged in the work of the team. The strongest bosses strike the perfect balance between personal availability and team autonomy. To achieve this balance consistently, great bosses use these three primary venues:

- ▶ Team Huddles
- ▶ Inclusive Staff Meetings
- ▶ Integrated Rounding

Team Huddles anticipate issues and problem-solve real time

Discussions of effective management practices tend to overdo sports analogies, but since we borrowed the term "huddle" from

football, thinking about what makes sports huddles effective —
and where we may have lost our way in translation in business
— seems appropriate.

Whether you are a personal fan or not, it is hard to argue with
the fact that Peyton Manning is one of the greatest professional
football players in history. Manning was great not only because
he was a talented quarterback but also because he was a gifted
leader who brought out the best in the entire team. Arguably, he
understood leadership as well as Peter Drucker, Jack Welch, or any
other management guru. And he especially understood what it
took to make the huddle before a key play successful.

> *"The most valuable player is the one that makes the most
> players valuable."* — *Peyton Manning*

That quote captures the essence of what makes a huddle successful. Huddles should be focused on pulling together to solve
immediate problems real-time, leveraging the unique strengths
different individuals bring to the team.

For perspective, Wikipedia defines huddle as: "an action of a
team gathering together, usually in a tight circle, to strategize,
motivate or celebrate." All three of those goals — to strategize,
motivate, and/or celebrate — are relevant to successful team
huddles in business. Yet many huddles I've seen operate in direct
opposition to those goals, and it's no wonder staff dread them so
much. In my work with work teams, I most often find that huddles
don't work because:

- ► They are too long.
- ► They try to cover too much territory.
- ► They are emotional downers.

First and foremost, huddles should unite and bring energy to a team as they start their shift or drive toward the successful completion of a project. Here are the three huddle characteristics I see that build energy and drive success.

1. Keep it Brief

Five minutes. That should be the goal for an effective team huddle. Staff members have lots to do, so they are ready to get to work. Always make the huddle a stand-up gathering in a hallway or common area to encourage brevity.

2. Keep it Focused on Today

Monthly staff meetings are the right place to deal with larger, longer-term issues facing the team. Huddles should be about the issues facing the team today (or the next few days for project-related huddles) and how they will confront them to be most successful.

Keeping the huddle brief and focused on today doesn't mean that the team should approach it in an informal, haphazard way. Brevity and focus require a little planning to be sure the right topics are covered in the right way.

3. Keep it Uplifting

Teams need to know where they are falling short and what they need to work on to improve. But the huddle is the wrong place to deal with longer-term problems that are challenging or discouraging. A manager announcing "we're still missing our customer satisfaction goals" leaves the team in a very different emotional place than "remember that our clients appreciate it when we use active listening to understand the concerns that are most important to them today."

Though many years ago, I still remember asking frontline staff in an organization that we were just starting to work with about their daily huddle. They replied, "Oh, you mean the 'daily beating!'" When I attended their huddle the next morning, I quickly understood where the pejorative name came from. The manager used the morning stand-up meeting to deal with everything the staff was doing wrong. While these issues needed to be addressed, berating the team immediately before sending them out to interact with and take care of customers was terrible timing.

Just like an inspiring coach, great leaders wrap up huddles and send their teams out on the field with a message of confidence, trust, and appreciation. My favorite model for this practice is Sgt. Phil Esterhaus (played by Michael Conrad) on the popular 1980s series *Hill Street Blues*. Sgt. Esterhaus always ended the team huddle with his signature line of support and advice, "Heh, let's be careful out there."

Huddles should motivate, clarify, and bring energy to the start of a shift or to a team working on a critical project. Remembering B.T.U. (which you might notice is the abbreviation for a measure of *energy*) — **brief**, **today,** and **uplifting** — is the best way to make a huddle powerful and most beneficial for your team.

Beyond these three foundational principles, here are additional ideas and issues to consider to make huddles work best for both bosses and their teams.

Form and frequency follow function

When you think of the classic huddle in business, most people imagine a group of staff members on the factory floor, a nursing unit, or similar work area at the beginning of a shift. A huddle at the beginning of every day works great in these situations, but not for every department. For teams whose daily work doesn't change as often, such as finance, human resources, or other support services, a daily huddle seems forced and a waste of time. In these circumstances, a regular huddle every few days or ad hoc huddles to deal with shifts in priorities work much better for everyone.

Stand up!

In many industries, the huddle is called a "stand up." And perhaps that name is more appropriate since it describes one of the key characteristics of success. When everyone stays standing, it clearly signals that the meeting will be brief. Standing vs. sitting also keeps the physical and mental energy and sense of urgency higher.

One day at a time

Effective huddles anticipate immediate roadblocks or challenges and problem-solve around them. Examples include unexpected staff call-offs, a breakdown in a key piece of equipment, or an unusual surge in volume related to a huge sale (in retail) or crisis/event (in service organizations). Longer range issues, of course, need to be dealt with by leadership and the team, but the huddle is the wrong place to get into lengthy, more complex conversations. Invariably, discussion goes too long, and staff members get frustrated.

A team sport

The best huddles encourage input from all members of the team. One of my favorite team huddle success stories comes from a director at Summa Health, who said she often approached the team ready to solve a looming staffing or process issue, only to be told, "The village has it handled!" You know the huddle is working when frontline team members form their own stand-up meeting to tackle an issue. That kind of cooperative, empowered problem-solving by frontline staff only happens when all staff feel encouraged to contribute.

Ditch the script

Planning ahead to make the huddle efficient and productive is one thing. Overly scripting the huddle with company platitudes or mumbo-jumbo is something else. Staff want the huddle to be real, not staged.

Several years ago, I was working with a very large, multi-state organization that wanted to use huddles to develop a more informed, engaged workforce. Unfortunately, their implementation plan significantly missed the mark. To make huddles consistent across the organization, every manager received a script to be read at the beginning of daily huddles. The managers who dutifully read the script as instructed got lots of eye rolls from their staff. But the impact on frontline employees was worse than just skepticism. The script made them feel like the people in the corporate office were completely out of touch with what was happening on the frontlines.

The lesson from this example goes well beyond just daily huddles. Smart organizations give middle managers a voice in communication strategies involving their team members. If an organization truly believes that they can't trust frontline bosses to say the right things to their teams without a script, they have the wrong individuals in those roles.

Huddle about the huddle

If huddles don't seem to be working for your team, you may be trying to force a round peg into a square hole. In the spirit you want to model in the huddle, ask your team for their suggestions and ideas on what would make the huddle most helpful. Don't be surprised if skeptics offer, "just stop holding huddles." Respectfully remind staff that the huddle can play a key role in consistent communication and the ability of the team to work well together. Then together reach a compromise that respects the team's ideas and the boss's resolve to make the huddle work for everyone.

Like any evidence-based leadership practice, the how and why behind huddles are much more important than the what in making them successful. A boss's determination to make huddles most beneficial usually means charting an adapted path and approach that fits the specific characteristics of the team's work. When done with intention, huddles not only drive efficiency but also create a structured space for open dialogue, fostering clearer communication and stronger connections across the team.

Leadership rounding keeps bosses connected and real

Theoretically, as bosses move up in an organization, they delegate more and more duties and tasks to those below them. But there is one responsibility that better bosses know they cannot delegate: their own personal visibility and connection to staff. The tie that leaders, especially senior executives, have with staff at all levels makes an invaluable impact on employee commitment, productivity, and loyalty. That's the power of effective leadership rounding.

> *"I have to be seen to be believed."* — *Queen Elizabeth II*

I first heard that quote several years ago during Queen Elizabeth's funeral. British commentators remarked that the limousine carrying her casket had been designed by the Queen personally to physically mirror that philosophy. The vehicle was specially equipped with large, clear glass windows on every side so she could be seen during her final ride through the streets of London.

The queen's quote stuck with me because it captures why leadership visibility is so essential and powerful — when done in the right way and in the right spirit.

Leadership rounding has been tagged with many different monikers, including LEAN's "Gemba walk" and Hewlett Packard's "management by walking around." I like to describe it as "integrated" because it's more effective when it creates synergistic connections among all of a boss's key constituencies: employees, customers, and colleagues.

But more important than what we call the practice, all successful leadership rounding approaches have one thing in common: they are about bosses effectively learning from front-line staff and customers, then using that knowledge to improve performance and the work environment. I've found the following ideas related to successful rounding especially important.

"Check *in* on staff, not *up* on staff"

Credit for this wonderful philosophy — and the clever phrase that captures its essence — goes to my friend Lanie Ward, the former chief nursing officer at Summa Health in Akron, OH. Lanie understood that the real power in senior leadership rounding with staff was in making meaningful connections with employees, not in evaluating their performance. (That is better left to their direct supervisor.) When bosses try to conflate gaining insights and expressing appreciation with assessing performance, staff usually only remember the evaluation part of their boss's time with them, often remarking, "It feels like they're only here because they don't trust us." Ouch. Obviously, that's not the impression we want increased leadership visibility to leave.

"How are *you* doing?" vs. "How are *we* doing?"

Several years ago, I had the privilege of being the keynote speaker for a series of quality forums held by Universal Health for their leadership teams. Individual hospital teams made mini presentations related to their performance improvement initiatives just prior to my keynote, so I benefited from hearing about their experiences in addition to sharing my ideas on improving engagement.

I still remember the executive team that shared insights on making leadership rounding on customers more powerful. Their efforts started with a list of questions posed to patients and family members about staff practices and behaviors, including hourly rounding, cleanliness, quietness, etc. They immediately ran up against a hesitance to open up. Research across industries tells us that customers are usually reluctant to talk about concerns while they are still with us. Why? Because they find it intimidating and are concerned about the potential for retaliation in some way.

This executive team found their conversations changed dramatically when they started by asking patients how *they* were doing rather than focusing on staff performance. When a level of trust and rapport was established, a question like, "Is there anything that could have been better or that we should change?" often elicited more candid responses.

A conversation, not an interrogation

In an effort to make rounding more "purposeful" and structured, I've seen companies develop and standardize questionnaires, then send bosses out with clipboards (or tablets) to talk with staff and customers. Their interactions usually end up seeming more like an interrogation than a conversation, and they gain far fewer insights into how people are really feeling. Open-ended questions that invite customers to share what has gone well — and what could be better — produce more valuable responses. Sometimes this approach takes a bit of encouragement and reassurance: "I know you said everything is going fine, but if you could change just one thing to make it even better, what would that be?"

In the same spirit of standardization, I've seen some companies try to track, chart, and graph discrete responses captured during rounding. The problem with this practice is that by design rounding conversations are *qualitative* research, not *quantitative*. Smart companies use the statistically valid results from engagement/satisfaction surveys to quantitatively measure customer and employee experience. Interested, connected bosses use rounding conversations to uncover the qualitative insights behind the numbers to identify real-time opportunities that address concerns or issues expressed by staff and customers.

Poor follow up squashes the benefits of rounding conversations

When bosses are not disciplined about following up with staff and customers on the problems that surface during rounding, credibility suffers. When I was starting a workforce culture assessment in a health system that had just launched standardized leader rounding on staff, I learned just how damaging poor follow up can be. This hospital's model had bosses visiting other colleagues' departments to increase understanding of issues across the leadership team. One of the questions on their pre-determined survey was, "Do you have the tools you need to do your job?" One of the managers we spoke with admitted how uncomfortable she felt when she asked a nurse that question during rounds. The nurse tersely replied, "No, we don't have access to the pulse oximeters we need to take care of the number of patients we have on our floor — just like I told the person who asked me that same question two weeks ago!"

If we can't respond to the issues identified during rounding, we shouldn't ask the question.

"Drive-by" rounds don't count

Perceptive bosses recognize that there are varying degrees of leadership visibility. Quickly walking through a unit and casually saying, "How's everybody doing today?" may seem friendly, but it doesn't advance your connection with your team. I've labeled that practice "drive-by" rounding, and its benefits are questionable. Most staff I've interviewed recognize that their boss can't always take time to stop and talk. But when their manager *never* takes time to stop and listen in an engaged way, waving as they walk by starts to feel disingenuous and dismissive of their real concerns.

Round to achieve a higher purpose

When leadership teams focus more on the needs of customers and team members, very positive things happen to reinforce a positive, performance-oriented culture. While the ultimate goal may be to improve results and success for the organization, rounding that starts with meaningful engagement is the most powerful, sustainable way to get there.

One of the most enlightening experiences I've ever had while rounding with a leader happened years ago at Jacobi Medical Center in The Bronx. One evening, I had the good fortune to meet and learn from Pedro Cineza, RN, a dedicated assistant director of nursing. I was rounding with Mr. Cineza during the evening/night shift to identify and better understand some of the unique struggles and opportunities to improve the patient experience on the third "tour."

As we visited the seven large medical/surgical units throughout the hospital, I watched something special happen as we walked on each floor. Mr. Cineza greeted each staff member by name and introduced them to me. Nurses, techs, housekeepers — he knew them all personally. And he wasn't simply reading the name badges. In fact, he pointed out to several staff members that their badge was not clearly visible.

I didn't keep count, but there were easily ten to fifteen staff members on each of the units we visited. That night, I'm sure, was not unique. So, when you do the math, you quickly realize that Mr. Cineza had a personal connection with hundreds of staff members throughout the house.

As we finished our rounds, I commented on how impressed — and heartened — I was that he knew everyone we encountered by name. He smiled and said, "When I step onto a unit, I want all of the staff members to be drawn to me, not to scatter."

At that moment, I came to appreciate another meaningful way for bosses to evaluate the effectiveness of their rounding. When you step into a unit or department, are staff drawn to you — or do you have to flush them out to have "purposeful" conversations? Their reaction speaks volumes about whether they feel supported or intimidated by your efforts to be more visible.

Leadership rounding done in a thoughtful, meaningful way can be a powerful strategy to improve both patient and employee engagement. Done wrong, it can undermine the trust and confidence that is so essential to building a strong, high-performance culture.

Staff meetings should be about building community, not just sharing information

"Another meeting?!"

It's a frustration I hear often. And for good reason. Meetings are often held for the wrong reasons, are poorly planned, and can be just plain boring. Back-to-back meetings without much time to shift gears or think in between is a particularly common problem for bosses in many companies.

But inclusive, open, and well-planned department staff meetings are one of the most powerful places to cultivate teamwork and trust across a team. Like so many long-standing, accepted management practices, the magic and key to success is in the *how* and *why* we deploy them.

First, if bosses believe that the primary purpose of a team meeting is to share information, they will continue to be disappointed in the lukewarm reception they get from their staff. Too many department meetings consist of 55 minutes of standard reports, recitation of new policies, and operational updates — followed by five minutes of, "Do you have any questions?" All this one-way communication sucks the very life out of meetings and discourages most staff members from speaking up.

If your goals are to improve staff engagement, teamwork and overall performance, here are ten tips to make team meetings more meaningful.

1.   Help them come prepared.

Effective meetings don't just happen without a little planning. Send a well-structured agenda a day or two ahead of time so everyone knows what to expect and can come prepared with ideas and questions on specific issues.

2. And help them leave energized.

Record key ideas, decisions, and next steps so that discussion feels more purposeful and action-oriented. Share the bullet-point summary with the entire team so that those who couldn't attend stay informed of important shared information.

3. Facilitate, don't dictate.

An effective meeting is about facilitated discussion, not staged presentation. That's a problem I've often heard called "death by PowerPoint." Part of effective facilitation is making sure everyone has the opportunity to contribute and that one or two strong individuals don't dominate discussion.

4. Invite senior leaders to join – occasionally.

Leader rounding and organization-wide town hall meetings are great. But if executives really want to hear from individual teams, there is no better venue than their staff meeting. Courageous, smart leaders proactively invite their bosses to attend their staff meetings every so often, especially when there is a major change or issue related to the department's work. For middle managers, having an executive attend their staff meeting offers the additional benefit of alignment up and down the leadership ladder.

5. Always share and discuss updates on key goals and priorities.

Simply posting quality metrics and customer experience results isn't enough. Successful bosses share and discuss results with their team on a monthly basis, giving staff the opportunity to celebrate success and course-correct together when results fall short of targets.

6. Break bread together.

This suggestion may sound trivial, but there is something about sharing food that brings people together. No big catering budget required; it can be as simple as stocking a basket with favorite candies or assigning responsibility for bringing treats to celebrate that month's birthdays.

7. Allow — even encourage — healthy, respectful venting.

Pretending that staff members don't get frustrated is naive. If you don't give them a safe place to express concerns and issues, they'll usually go underground and vent unproductively to each other — or even worse, to customers. Staff meetings should be a safe space where employees can discuss their frustrations, then quickly transition to discussions about how to solve or reduce those frustrations.

8. Use discussion at staff meetings to spur performance improvement.

Research confirms that having a say in how important work gets done is a major source of satisfaction for employees. Including operational issues on the agenda that are good candidates for improvement is a great way to get the entire team involved in early brainstorming and discussion.

9. Spotlight great work by individual team members.

Supportive bosses allow talented team members to share responsibility for making team meetings successful. Be sure to spotlight reports from performance improvement teams and updates on key initiatives driven by team members.

10. Strive for a 50/50 communication ratio.

That means staff have at least as much time to offer ideas and ask questions as bosses do to share information. Of all these tips, this simple ratio makes the biggest difference in energizing staff meetings and helping employees embrace initiatives that will make the team most successful.

Staff meetings should be forums where employees come together to share ideas and support one another rather than staid, mandatory events that they reluctantly attend. By shifting their mindset, successful bosses invigorate team meetings to build teamwork and trust.

CHAPTER 12

EMPOWER:
Why Giving Staff Voice Helps a Team —and Its Boss

E mpowerment is a frequently vaunted goal for high-func-
tioning teams in today's leadership literature. But while the
term is commonly cited and extolled, I'm not sure it adequately
describes the true strength and advantages of the philosophy. If
you click on the thesaurus in Microsoft Word for synonyms to
empower, you'll find a much more robust list that reflects the full
power of empowerment: *inspire, embolden, encourage, galvanize,
and energize.*

There is ample evidence supporting the wisdom of empowering a team. Dr. Christina Maslach's research on the root causes of burnout is a prime example; giving employees more voice and control makes a major difference in how they feel about their work. But there is another significant benefit to empowerment that doesn't get as much attention: giving staff more say and control in problem solving and decision making makes life better and more successful for *bosses*, too.

At the heart of contemporary process improvement methodologies is the idea that the best solutions emerge when they come from the people closest to the work. But the advantages of involving frontline workers go beyond just the insights they offer around how to best fix problems. When they are involved in improving aspects of operations, production, and service, they have a greater stake in the eventual solution. Rather than bosses having to impose another set of new policies and procedures on employees, they own their solution and are more committed to making it work.

With an empowered team, the work environment begins to sound like nirvana. But wise bosses understand that there's a catch. True empowerment isn't simply bestowed on a team by their boss; it happens only when individuals and teams want to be empowered. In other words, the reality that "you can lead a horse to water, but you can't make him drink" applies to empowerment.

When staff take ownership for providing the very best product or service to customers, there are multiple benefits. Structured opportunities for shared decision-making and small-group problem solving help instill a sense of responsibility among team members. But these important efforts can be undermined if a leader doesn't support empowerment literally every day in the language she uses with her team.

The article "Can Your Employees Really Speak Freely?" [17] from a 2016 issue of the Harvard Business Review provides a thoughtful, research-based assessment of what encourages and inhibits open communication and collaborative problem-solving in organizations. Authors James R. Detert and Ethan R. Burris describe the two "F" factors usually at the heart of employees' reluctance to speak up: *fear* and *futility*. Simply, employees have to believe that there won't be retribution if they speak up and that their ideas will actually make a difference.

While there is no absolute, fail-safe path for creating an environment where employees enthusiastically embrace openness and transparency, it is also true that to promote a culture of trust and frankness, bosses have to start somewhere. Here are six straightforward statements that capture and reinforce a culture of true empowerment.

"What's been your experience?"

Consistently asking employees their opinions on both routine and more substantive issues is one of the most clear-cut ways to build a culture of empowerment. Of course, when they tell you what they think, you have to be willing to consider their advice or the inquiry is empty and meaningless.

Early in my career as an executive, I had a long-term manager leave. While this manager was technically competent and hardworking, I was shocked to learn from frontline supervisors in the department that a caustic atmosphere permeated the work group because of the director's fear-based management style. I struggled to understand how I could have missed this. In looking for ways I could avoid a problem like this in the future, I sought the confidential advice of a savvy HR director I respected. After listening to my story and appreciating my interest in getting open feedback from staff members, she matter-of-factly said, "Why don't you ask them?"

At the time, I remember thinking that the answer was more simplistic than I expected. But while I had my doubts about whether staff members would really speak honestly to the boss, I took her advice to heart and started asking staff members more often to tell me how they were doing. To my amazement, it worked. And the more I did it, the more insightful — and re-spectful — the feedback became.

In retrospect, the suggestion to "just ask" was one of the best pieces of advice I've ever received on how to create an atmosphere of openness and transparency. I've also learned, however, that it only works when staff members' frankness and courage to speak up is rewarded with respect and a non-punitive response. If a boss is only hearing "yeah, things are great," he knows there is more work to do to truly create a culture where everyone can candidly share both their compliments and criticisms.

"I trust you."

Knowing that the boss respects their experience and judgment regarding both problems and opportunities is essential for em-ployees to take bigger risks and voice their ideas.

"Your solution is better than mine."

A boss that encourages employees to step up, take owner-ship, and be part of the solution must be a confident, humble leader. Especially newer managers sometimes make the mistake of thinking that they must have all the answers to be seen as a strong leader. When they don't, they fear it makes them look weak and ineffective. But the opposite is usually true. Bosses who turn to their teams for input and then acknowledge that their solution is much better than the one they would have crafted create confidence and a willingness to take greater accountability for the results of the team.

"I was wrong."

When a boss believes — or indirectly communicates — that he is always right, staff stop offering new ideas that are different from his beliefs. A willingness to admit fault or error can be especially tough for newer managers to embrace as they struggle to be the boss to an experienced, strong-willed team. "Will it make me look weak or ineffective?" is always in the back of their mind.

Admitting that you're wrong does much more than just convey a sense of humbleness. It also sends the important message that *it is okay to be wrong*. Innovation is widely accepted as an essential core competency for organizations in today's rapidly changing and competitive environment, and one of the essential elements of innovation is a willingness to try lots of new things, expecting many of them to fail. Being wrong and denying it destroys trust; being wrong and learning from it is a sign of mature, healthy leadership.

"Let's talk about why that didn't work."

Sometimes just like bosses, employees don't have the best answers, either individually or collectively. Astute bosses recognize that making mistakes is part of the learning process. Unless they are careless or malicious, mistakes deserve constructive feedback, not punishment. That said, good leaders also are there to guide and provide advice to members of their teams to prevent disastrous mistakes that could cause irreparable damage.

Some of the most fruitful, trust-building conversations I've had with staff were at times when I needed to explain why their point of view didn't take into account all of the factors related to an issue. Invariably, they better understood and accepted why we were taking a particular approach — and I understood their ideas and concerns at a deeper level.

"Thank you."

A culture of acknowledgment and appreciation when employees step up and go that extra mile ensures they will come back tomorrow ready to do the same thing again. I always cringe when I hear organizations try to make recognition a "program." There's nothing wrong with structured rewards, but they don't take the place of a boss frequently and sincerely looking an employee in the eyes and simply saying those two powerful words ... *thank you* for what you've done and the difference you've made.

If we want our "villages" to step up, consistently take ownership for improving results, and truly feel empowered, bosses must be conscious of the messages they're sending and the implications of the actions they're taking every day. Rather than something that bosses concede to staff, true empowerment is a mutually beneficial philosophy that creates a superior work environment for both frontline staff and bosses.

CHAPTER 13

ALIGN:

Great Bosses Provide Clarity and Direction

The last chapter emphasized the benefits of empowerment and giving employees a voice, so you may be surprised to learn that this chapter — the Align component of the T.E.A.M. Model — professes that effective bosses also sometimes tell staff what to do. In practice, the best bosses balance employee problem solving with clear directions on priorities for the team. To succeed at the latter, two major factors come into play:

- ► How goals are structured and communicated
- ► How the team embraces specific practices to achieve individual goals

To address both of these successfully, let's look at one of the most common acronyms related to goal-setting, S.M.A.R.T., and adapt the model to focus more on using goals to change behavior.

If you've worked in any large organization, you've probably been encouraged to write S.M.A.R.T. goals. George Doran, Arthur Miller, and James Cunningham introduced this easy-to-remember acronym in a 1981 issue of *Management Review*.[18] While many authors and practitioners have adapted the concept, the original acronym stood for: **S**pecific, **M**easurable, **A**ssignable, **R**ealistic, and **T**ime-Bound.

The trio created a model with serious staying power in management practice. When I speak to groups and ask, "Has anyone heard of 'SMART' goals?", almost every hand in the room goes up.

Despite its memorability and simplicity, the SMART goal approach by design has limitations. As suggested in the authors' original article title — "There's a SMART Way to Write Management Goals and Objectives" — the focus of the original model was on the content of the *written* goal itself. It didn't address how to structure and communicate goals effectively so that they actually influence behaviors and outcomes. That requires a different set of considerations and questions:

> ► *Why is the goal important to our customers, our organization, and to members of our team?*

> ► *Is everyone on board regarding the specific practices that will help us achieve this goal?*

> ► *Can we achieve the goal given the resources we have for implementation?*

> ► *How do we know if we're making progress?*

> ► *Do we celebrate when we succeed together? And do we course-correct when we fall short?*

Our adapted S.M.A.R.T. goal model, which focuses more on implementation and making goals relevant for staff, changes the "M", "A", and "T" in the original model and expands how we think about the "S."

Specific

While there are a few variations on the original S.M.A.R.T. goals model, the "S" always stands for "specific." Writing a SMART goal that is specific means that all aspects of the goal are clearly defined and that it answers the standard 5 Ws (who, what, when, where, and why). But even when a well-written goal is specific, it still usually focuses on what you want the end result to be, not on how you'll get there.

> *Clear departmental leading goals help achieve a company's lagging goals*

In their best-selling book *The Four Disciplines of Execution*, Sean Covey, Chris McChesney, and Jim Huling describe the importance of setting both "lagging" and "leading" goals to change performance. Lagging goals, which are the ones companies usually set, look in the rear-view mirror and measure results (for example, our operating margin last quarter or quality scores last year).

Leading goals, on the other hand, target specific predictive behaviors that will lead to better performance and achieving the company's lagging goals. While you can think of them like action plans, leading goals go a step further by identifying specific metrics or activities to track in implementation.

For example, a strong, specific lagging goal for an individual hotel guest service team might be:

> *To improve customer loyalty, increase "I felt valued and recognized as a platinum rewards member" score on customer experience survey from 78.5 to 81.0 by end of third quarter.*

While this goal flags guest experience as a priority for staff, it does little to help them collectively understand what needs to change to achieve the goal. Here is where a leading goal is beneficial:

> *To improve customer loyalty and satisfaction, check reward member status first at check-in. Immediately thank the guest for their status and extend a friendly "Welcome back!" before completing the remainder of the process. Achieve 100% compliance for all guests by end of second quarter.*

The specificity of a well-structured leading goal clarifies practice and/or process changes that will be necessary to achieve a lagging goal. This approach helps each member of the team better understand their personal responsibilities in achieving better outcomes. In this example, it emphasizes that the team will have to pay attention to how often they are welcoming and thanking a premium rewards member, not just the score on the "I felt valued" satisfaction survey question.

> *Strong leading goals focus on quality, not just quantity, of implementation*

While it is important to quantify and track the frequency of key practices and behaviors, leading goals often have qualitative components to watch, as well. In this example, how the welcome and thanks are expressed is at least as important as if and when it happens.

Meaningful

"Please help me connect the dots!"

In our work with frontline staff, this plea is one of the most common ones we hear. With new protocols, quality and service requirements, and regulations shifting constantly in most industries, staff understandably struggle to make sense of all these changes. That's why setting goals is just step one. Linking them to organizational *purpose* and exploring them in ways that are *meaningful* to your team is essential to achieving them.

In today's metrics-driven world, it is easy for even the most passionate, purpose-focused employee to quickly become obsessed with the numbers. Daily volume targets. Safety incidents per month. Customer experience top box scores. Chasing the numbers can become all-consuming.

Sadly, "money" is too often our answer when staff ask why tracking all these numbers really matters. Yes, companies of course must worry about operating margins and cash flow. But when we set goals that are based on something beyond just dollars, employees embrace them more enthusiastically. This principle is especially important for the next generation of workers, who care deeply about doing important work and making a difference.

So, rather than simply tracking the numbers and trends, let's consider the meaning and significance behind goals, even when on the surface they are indeed at least partially about money. Below are tips for structuring and communicating more meaningful goals.

1. Begin goals with brief purpose phrases that usually start with "to," such as:

> ► *To reduce inconvenience for our customers, fully implement new triage system for routing call center incoming calls, reducing hold times by 25% by Q'IV.*

> ► *To improve the safety of our employees, launch revised high reliability training for all manufacturing managers and staff by Q'II, achieving 100% participation in workshops by Q'IV.*

> ► *To improve employee experience and well-being, increase senior leadership rounding to every month in all key divisions, with the goal of increasing engagement scores by a minimum of 10% in all areas.*

2. Use storytelling to get beyond the numbers and emphasize the meaningful impact compassionate care has on patients' lives.

In chapter 9 we explored how storytelling can help staff connect to purpose. Stories also help them appreciate and commit to achieving meaningful goals.

3. Recognize team members' specific contributions that help achieve team goals.

Specific, individualized recognition helps reduce burnout. It is also a powerful way to reinforce staff's efforts to achieve important goals that make a meaningful difference for customers and for the team.

Research tells us that losing a sense of purpose in our work is one of the major contributing factors to burnout. Goals that are meaningful and create a shared sense of purpose across the team are good for our customers. They're also good for frontline staff and leaders.

Agreed-Upon

Even the best crafted, precisely-targeted organizational goals are ineffective unless they are embraced by individuals and the entire team responsible for implementing the tactics to achieve them. That's why the "A" in the adapted S.M.A.R.T. goals model represents "agreed-upon."

The first, most important step in setting goals that are enthusiastically adopted by teams is to pay attention to two of the other components in our S.M.A.R.T. goals model: making goals *meaningful* and *realistic*. Tying a goal to the core purpose of the organization's work helps make its achievement more important. Even financial goals can be linked to the short- and long-term fiscal health of the organization and its ability to continue to invest in technology and services that will ultimately improve quality and customer experience. Additionally, to be well accepted by teams, the path to success has to be reasonable and realistic.

With that foundation, here are several tips for gaining agreement on goals that will help support their achievement.

Involve team members in crafting leading goals and tactical plans

Leading goals help teams meet larger organizational metrics. Frontline leaders can create support for these goals by involving their teams in the problem-solving that helps set them.

Spend time talking about goals, not just posting them

Organizations and department leaders too often distribute well-written goals — either via email or by tacking them on a bulletin board — without giving teams the chance to really understand their intent. The opportunity to ask questions and to discuss how the goal will be achieved is crucial for staff to truly embrace the objective and commit to its success.

Celebrate success; course-correct for shortfalls

Discussing a goal once isn't enough to sustain ongoing staff support. Updating plans to achieve departmental goals has to be a regular occurrence at staff meetings, during rounding with staff, and at huddles.

"Agreed-upon" is all about increasing employees' sense of ownership and commitment to the achievement of operational, quality, service, and financial goals. The litmus test for optimal team endorsement can be summed up in one question to staff: Is this *our* team's goal for improving performance or *their* (management's) goal to meet a company target? The answer says a lot about not just goal setting but also organizational culture.

Realistic

"I believe that this nation should commit itself to achieving the goal, before this decade is out, of landing a man on the moon and returning him safely to the Earth."

This quote from President John F. Kennedy's speech to a joint session of Congress on May 25, 1961, is perhaps the most often cited example of the philosophy that when you set stretch goals, amazing things can happen. And who doesn't want to accomplish amazing things?

So, the fact that the "R" in our smarter S.M.A.R.T. goals model stands for "realistic" may be surprising. Realistic sounds so safe ... run-of-the-mill ... even boring. Don't we want bigger, inspiring, stretch goals? Maybe even "B.H.A.G.s"?

Even if you haven't read the best-selling business book *Built to Last* by Jim Collins and Jerry Porras, you've probably heard about "big, hairy, audacious goals." And the first example of a B.H.A.G. cited by Collins and Porras is, of course, President Kennedy's bold man-on-the-moon goal.

Does our suggestion that goals should be realistic mean that we believe B.H.A.G.s aren't useful, or worse, just pipe dreams? Not at all. It simply means that to be realistic, B.H.A.G.s require B.H.A.R.s — big, hairy, audacious *resources*.

What Makes a Goal Realistic — or Unrealistic?

While everyone quotes the man-on-the-moon ambition in President Kennedy's speech to Congress, the sentence immediately following that statement was arguably just as important: *"I therefore ask the Congress, above and beyond the increases I have earlier requested for space activities, to provide the funds which are needed to meet the following national goals...."*

No goal, in and of itself, is either realistic or unrealistic. Leaders need to ask one straightforward question to determine reasonableness: *Can we and will we devote sufficient resources to achieving the goal?*

Kennedy's bold challenge to put a man on the moon was both aspirational and inspirational. Its primary purpose was to rally the support of the American people, and more importantly, the Congress to fund the goal's achievement. Remember that the space program at the time was a matter of national pride. We had to beat the Russians, and we were behind in the early 1960s.

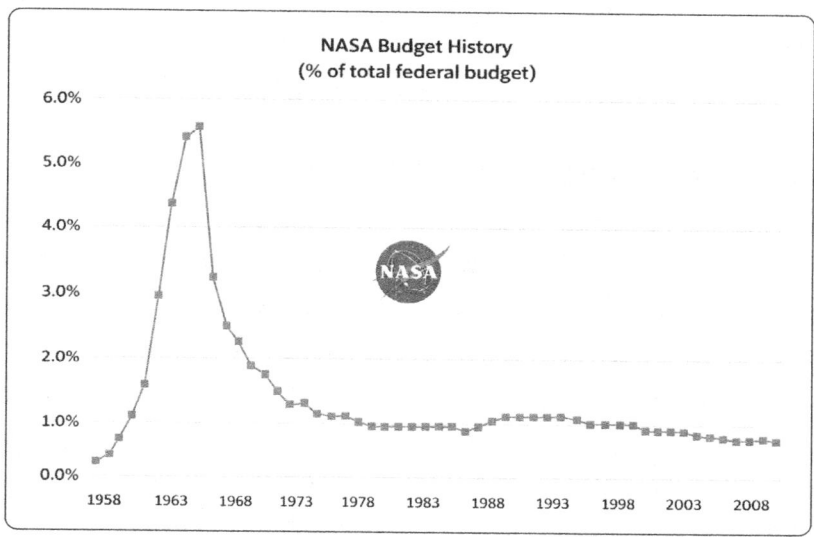

This chart illustrates how significantly resources often have to be redirected to achieve a B.H.A.G. NASA's annual budget in 1961 was $744 million. By 1966, at its peak, the annual NASA budget had reached $5.9 billion, an increase of nearly 700%. As the line graph shows, the increase in the share of total federal spending for NASA in the 1960s was even more dramatic and illustrates another important point: effective planning and goal-setting is about prioritization. Resources are not unlimited, so focusing time and spending in one area usually means sacrifices in others.

Here are three principles that organizations and bosses follow for setting aggressive but realistic goals that are achievable.

Recognize that not every goal can be a B.H.A.G.

Stretch goals are fine, but not every goal in every area can be a stretch. Setting aggressive goals in a few areas and devoting adequate resources to achieving them is better than spreading resources too thin. Keep in mind that stretch goals that are not adequately funded can shift from inspirational to demoralizing for those involved.

A stretch for one unit may be a cakewalk for another

Organization-wide goals for quality, safety, or service metrics may be reasonable, but leaders often need to analyze and adjust them to be realistic for individual units. This is especially true for customer experience goals. It is fine to set a goal of reaching the 75th percentile rank for an operating unit that has been at the 60th percentile. But for another unit at the 25th percentile with a more challenging customer population, that goal in a single year would be extremely difficult.

Industry data helps determine the resources required to hit a goal

In some areas, using industry benchmark data can help teams assess just how challenging a goal will be. For example, customer satisfaction research companies can tell you how many of their client organizations, on average, moved performance by specific amounts depending on their starting points.

Linking the allocation of resources to the achievement of stretch goals is essential. Well-intentioned "inspirational" goals quickly become disheartening for teams when hampered by too few resources to achieve them.

Tracked

How often do organizations develop and share annual goals at the start of a new year, then barely talk about them with work teams until twelve months later when posting final results? Is it any wonder teams often miss the target when they don't consistently track goal performance?

Successful bosses help teams stay focused on achieving critical operational, financial, and quality goals every day. Monitoring, sharing, and discussing progress throughout the year are all essential to making that happen. That's why the "T" in our model stands for "tracked."

The following five practices help supportive bosses track and report goal performance while engaging staff and improving results.

Go beyond simply posting results

Updated reports from quality and customer satisfaction surveys, as well as other operational metrics, have to be more than just another piece of paper posted on a staff bulletin board. Great leaders encourage team dialogue about results during every department meeting, allowing sufficient time to really discuss the implications of the results.

Celebrate success

Too often we hear frontline staff complain, "They only notice when something goes wrong." Supportive bosses notice and take time to acknowledge and celebrate success along the way, which reinforces best practices and superior performance. Plus, it just feels good!

Course-correct for shortfalls

When results fall short of expectations, high-performing teams seek to understand why. Too often, bosses simply say, "we must do better" without understanding the root cause of the performance gap. Underlying that flawed thinking is the assumption that the team is doing the right things, but they are not doing them well enough. Many times, the real problem may be that the practices implemented to achieve the goal are misaligned. Only when a team understands that a change in course is necessary will results improve.

A picture is worth a thousand numbers

Straightforward graphs or charts that quickly illustrate the trend in performance are far more powerful than lots of numbers and words. Additionally, great bosses and teams look for the details behind the graphs to better understand why performance is trending in a certain direction.

Tell stories to make the results real

Numbers are important, but the impact those numbers have on customers' lives is what really matters. When I was a young product manager at Purina, we took a very disciplined approach to tracking shipments, distribution, market share, and financial returns. It took a powerful story during a customer focus group discussion to remind me why the company existed and the obligation I had to our loyal customers. One elderly woman spoke up early in the group, and her comments provided the perfect context and foundation for the rest of the discussion.

"My cat Sam means everything to me," she shared. "Since my husband died, he's the only member of my immediate family I have left. I feed him Cat Chow because I know Purina is a company who cares as much about my Sam as I do."

When goals are well-structured and focused on meaningful priorities, they play an important role in helping individuals and teams find purpose in their daily work. Frontline bosses help their teams achieve those goals not just because it's what their bosses up the ladder expect. They know that goals are a powerful way to bring people together, encourage teamwork, and build a strong sense of community around shared aspirations.

CHAPTER 14

MENTOR:
Developing Individuals
Builds Strong Teams

Helping individuals fully develop their strengths and achieve fulfilling personal success is, I believe, one of the most gratifying and important responsibilities of effective bosses. Unfortunately, it has become one of the most neglected aspects of leadership. That reality is not entirely the fault of hard-working middle managers. It is tough to devote the time and energy to helping individuals be at their best when most of your day is spent attending meetings with your peers or superiors, completing reports, and putting out fires.

Although there's often little time left for mentorship, it's a critical practice that pays dividends in the long run. Research by Gallup demonstrates why interactions between bosses and their teams are so critical:[19]

- ► Employees who report receiving meaningful feedback in the past week are five times more likely to be engaged

- ► Companies that prioritize feedback have 14.9% lower turnover rates

- ► Employees who receive daily feedback are 3.6 times more likely to be motivated to do outstanding work compared to those who receive it annually

That's why great bosses find ways to mentor individual members of their team and help them grow personally and professionally. They make time for this important work for two primary reasons. First, connected bosses find personal satisfaction in mentoring others, so they *want* to make time more than they feel like they *have* to make time. And second, they integrate consistent feedback into their day-to-day responsibilities so that it doesn't feel like extra work.

Gallup's studies and my experience working alongside strong bosses reveal that smaller, more frequent actions have a bigger impact on employees' engagement, development, and sense of self-worth than major, time consuming "events" like an annual performance appraisal. In my work with frontline leaders, they tell me the annual performance appraisal process is one of their most burdensome, frustrating responsibilities. Company senior leaders usually know it isn't working, either. I've made a point over the past ten years to ask C-suite executives a simple question: is the annual appraisal process worth the time and expense that you devote to it? Only once have I had a CEO answer yes — but the people closer to the frontlines in that organization quietly told me they didn't find it important or useful.

The three components of the T.E.A.M. model's "mentor" section impact individual staff members' development in different but complementary ways, collectively addressing the six root causes of burnout both directly and indirectly.

Frequent Feedback

For busy managers to provide more frequent feedback to team members, these conversations can't be an "event" every time. Instead, mentorship needs to become *how* effective bosses do their job every day rather than an extra list of tasks piled onto other responsibilities. That doesn't mean time with individual members of their team is left to chance. These interactions must be intentional and — because everyone's time is limited — efficient.

Frequent feedback is most effective when it's ...

- ► **Balanced** (incorporating both positive comments as well as constructive criticism)

- ► **Consistent** (so that the feedback becomes expected rather than an occasional surprise)

- ► **Relevant** (focused on specific behaviors or contributions by an employee)

The idea of balanced feedback and how to think about it is captured in the well-documented five-to-one golden ratio. This research-based strategy reveals the power of five positive comments for every one criticism in high-performing organizations. This practice and the underlying research were cited in a 2013 Harvard Business Review article by Jack Zenger and Joseph Folkman, "The Ideal Praise-to-Criticism Ratio."[20]

Qualitatively, in our work with teams, we've observed and heard from frontline staff that more praise than criticism works for three major reasons.

1.   More praise reinforces positive contributions

Whether the carrot or the stick is more effective in changing behavior is a centuries-old debate. But there is no doubt that positive reinforcement encourages the practices and behaviors that we know improve customer experience and the overall quality of products and services. But we've seen praise do more than that. Staff who feel appreciated and recognized are more likely to go above-and-beyond to support their colleagues and customers in ways that differentiate great companies from good ones.

2.   More praise makes criticism more palatable and powerful

While it may seem counterintuitive, one of the most important reasons to provide more positive recognition is to make negative feedback more effective. Staff in organizations where leaders only point out the problems or shortcomings become more discouraged and less likely to go above-and-beyond. Providing balanced feedback better positions teams to both receive and embrace constructive criticism.

3.   More praise builds a culture of strength-development rather than weakness-obsession

Marcus Buckingham and Curt Coffman's 1999 best-seller *First Break All the Rules: What Great Managers Do Differently*[21] is the leadership bible for those of us who believe developing staff member's strengths (rather than trying to fix their weaknesses) is more effective — and makes work a lot more enjoyable. A culture of praise and appreciation is one of the key ways managers emphasize and leverage employees' strengths every day.

The five-to-one ratio is a powerful way for bosses to informally self-assess how close they are to providing balanced feedback to their team, but there can be a flaw in the way people *think about* the underlying value in five-to-one. By definition, this leadership principle focuses on quantity. But balanced feedback works best when bosses develop a mindset and bias toward recognition quality. Paying attention to the numbers is beneficial only to the extent that it forces us to recognize how seldom we might be providing positive feedback to our teams.

Difficult conversations test even the most experienced, talented bosses

While positive feedback is powerful, sometimes bosses have to have difficult conversations with team members regarding problematic behaviors or actions. Among the long list of demanding responsibilities facing frontline leaders, initiating difficult conversations with staff is one of the most dreaded. It's also one of the most important skills to develop.

Here are eight tips to make difficult conversations more effective, whether they are with your team, peers, bosses, or even customers. Steps one through four prepare you for the conversation and make the actual interaction more productive.

1.   Start with a clear, results-focused purpose for the conversation.

Too often, we approach all challenging conversations like our most dreaded scenario: having to fire someone or eliminate their job. The problem is that those encounters are not conversations. Rather, they are structured to deliver bad news in the most humane way possible, with little room for discussion or compromise.

The bigger missed opportunity is a straightforward conversation that helps an employee see their weaknesses, blind spots, and areas for personal improvement. Focusing on the purpose of the conversation and the results we hope to achieve helps us set the right tone and craft the right approach. Having these conversations earlier and more often may also help us avoid more agonizing conversations later.

2.   Put yourself in the other person's shoes.

Yes, empathy can and should play a role in difficult encounters. According to Forbes, research shows that empathy can be the most important leadership skill.[22] In challenging conversations, thinking about the issue you're addressing from the other person's perspective helps anticipate possible objections and craft fair, effective responses.

3.   Imagine the best possible outcome, then work backwards.

In an ideal world, how do you and the other person feel at the end of your conversation? Has it increased their resolve to take positive next steps or caused them to further disengage and resist change? Contemplating the desired outcome helps to prioritize both what you want to say and how you want to say it.

4.   Plan, prepare, and practice.

Confronting tough, divisive issues tests even the most adept, experienced communicators. They know success relies not just on an innate ability to initiate difficult discussions but also on their preparation. Consider sharing the background of a difficult conversation with one or two trusted confidants to test-drive your plan. This important step does more than surface ideas that you hadn't considered. Talking through your approach also makes you more confident and comfortable, which ultimately benefits both you and your employee.

   With good preparation, the likelihood that those difficult conversations go well increases significantly. Here are four additional tips to think about during the discussion.

5.   Don't start with "This is a difficult conversation for me to have with you."

Remember that the conversation isn't just about you and your resolve to address a difficult issue or situation. Be careful about opening statements that immediately put the other person on the defensive. This misstep can make them less likely to consider your ideas and change behaviors that will make them more successful.

6. Chart your course but be ready to tack to changing winds.

Being prepared doesn't mean being unyielding in your approach to the conversation. If it's truly a conversation, listening carefully to the other person's thoughts and reactions helps you respond more effectively and appropriately. Your ability to confidently and appropriately adjust course mid-conversation is largely dependent on how well you've prepared in steps one through four.

7. Control your emotions, but don't completely hide them.

I often tell leaders that losing control of your emotions means that you've lost control of a conversation. Lashing out in anger, disgust, or opposition doesn't advance the goals or purpose of any conversation. However, that doesn't mean you shouldn't let the other person know how you feel about a situation in a respectful way. Disappointment, concern, frustration, and disagreement — when expressed fairly and constructively — can all help the other person recognize the importance of an issue and where you stand on the need to change.

8. Provide support post-conversation.

If your goal is to change a behavior, follow-up support and continued assessment are necessary to achieve real, sustainable results. That said, be sure to make it clear that the responsibility to change is primarily theirs, not yours.

Initiating difficult conversations is a critical part of being a strong leader. Even when the news or issue is tough to hear, employees respect supportive bosses' willingness and ability to have these uncomfortable conversations in respectful ways that help them improve and be more successful.

Development Dialogues

Supporting frontline staff and staying connected to what they're feeling has never been more important. As the workforce has emerged from arguably the most disruptive worldwide crisis in our lifetime, the COVID-19 pandemic, many employees have adjusted the way they think about work-life balance and what's most important to them. Research shows this is especially true for the younger Millennial and GenZ generations.

Unlike the traditional performance appraisal meeting, the Development Dialogue is all about listening. Gallup calls these "stay conversations." But whatever you call them, they are all about understanding each employee's personal goals, concerns, and ideas. A dialogue about their future with the organization has never been so important. Asking an employee, "How are you doing?" is a reasonable first step. But that question alone, which often seems rhetorical, is hardly enough.

These five questions can help open a more meaningful dialogue.

> ► *What do you find most fulfilling in your job?*

> ► *And, what do you find most frustrating?*

> ► *Which accomplishments are you most proud of?*

> ► *How can your experience and skills contribute in an even bigger way to our success going forward?*

> ► *How can I and other members of the team best support you right now?*

Because of the long-term impact of the pandemic and changing attitudes about the nature and purpose of work, people are at a different place — personally and professionally — than they've ever been before. Empathetic bosses know that opening honest, forward-looking conversations with each individual can be one of the most important gifts a leader can offer to their team.

Observation

In addition to supporting individual employees' goals, helping them be successful, and creating strong teamwork, a boss's ultimate responsibility to customers is making sure that staff are doing the right things in the right way every day. Assessing individual staff members' competencies and compliance works best when you are regularly in the trenches to observe both their strengths and weaknesses.

In my work with organizations, we use a qualitative, field-tested survey process we call the "Staff and Leader Experience Snapshot" to help companies better understand their cultural strengths, weaknesses, and specific ways to improve staff engagement. One of our focus group questions to frontline staff is especially revealing.

What happens to lower performers on your team?

Answers range from "someone talks to them to help them do better" to "nothing." More revealing than their spoken answers are their non-verbals. You can guess which answer is accompanied by eye rolling and a resigned tone.

Conscientious bosses who care about staff engagement are sometimes reluctant to have frank conversations with lower performers. "I can't afford to lose anyone right now," is an understandable concern.

But lack of fairness in the workplace is one of the six root causes of employee burnout. When your best employees feel like not everyone is held equally accountable, that's perceived as not fair. And, along with other factors, that perceived unfairness can contribute to a good staff member's decision to look elsewhere.

These five practices help staff feel like everyone is treated equitably and fairly.

Lax accountability hurts your stars most

Lack of performance and accountability impacts the success of an entire team. But in terms of burnout and engagement, the people you want to keep most may be at the highest risk of resigning. Eventually, stars can reach a point of feeling, "why should I bust my butt when others don't contribute in the same way?" Recognizing their contributions both privately and publicly can moderate these feelings. But ultimately, holding everyone to reasonable, appropriate standards helps the team be at their best.

Make expectations clear

It's easy to be clear about the straightforward rules of the workplace: attendance, tardiness, documentation, etc. But more important are the rules about how we treat each other and the customers we serve. Connected leaders set aside time during staff meetings, huddles, and rounding to talk about organizational values. They tell stories about staff members going above and beyond to serve customers and their colleagues. And they share their personal aspirations and priorities about the way work gets done.

Strong leaders recognize that they share responsibility for poor individual performance within their work groups. The first step in leader accountability is setting clear expectations and goals.

Broach the subject of poor performance early.

Lynn Dull was the first person to share with me a very important leadership principle: *what you permit, you promote*. That philosophy was key to the establishment of a strong, accountable culture at BJC HealthCare's Progress West Hospital, where I had the good fortune to work with Lynn and the team as they opened their new hospital. The longer you wait to talk to a lower performer about their deficiencies, the more you communicate to them that their actions are acceptable. More concerning is the fact that you're sending the same message to the rest of the team.

Ask why

Effective leaders seek to understand the reasons behind poor performance. Opening the door to dialogue around performance may uncover structural or workforce culture issues that are inhibiting a team member from being at their best. While leaders intellectually recognize that burnout is rampant today, we sometimes hesitate to admit that it may be a primary driver behind lower performance. Dialogues that respectfully address these issues acknowledge that the environment in which the individual works affects performance just as much as individual factors.

Look for opportunities to reinforce positive contributions

Every individual on a work team has to feel some sense of hope that they can succeed. That's why leaders should go out of their way to look for positive contributions — even though they may seem small — among staff members who are struggling. It's especially important to recognize any changed behavior that you have coached an employee to work on.

Occasionally, I'll have a manager we're working with admit that they just can't find anything positive to say to an employee. Of course, that should tell you something. Effective leadership and change management theory tells us to pay attention to both the "skill" and "will" aspects of success. If employees lack skills, we should support them in getting better. If they don't have the will to contribute, ignore organizational values, and/or don't respect colleagues or patients, it is time to help them move along.

Among the four major components of the T.E.A.M. leadership framework, the time and effort you devote to mentoring individual employees can be the most powerful driver of success for you and your team. It also is often the most easily neglected. This leadership oversight, whether under-prioritized or simply under-appreciated, can create unexpected problems for bosses given the expectations of today's workforce. Recent studies show that the next generation of employees want and need constructive feedback more than their older colleagues.[23] Personal development is so important to Millennials and GenZers that they'll leave jobs where they don't feel like they're getting the mentoring they need to improve and progress.

Beyond the benefits for your staff, mentoring also can be one of the most personally gratifying aspects of being a boss. Helping others develop their own leadership skills leaves a lasting imprint on the personal success of others and on the organizations they'll serve for years to come.

CONCLUSION

As you've read this book and reflected on what it takes to be a great boss, I hope you've come to an important conclusion: becoming a better boss isn't easy. Yes, some of the lessons are straightforward and obvious. For example, effective bosses don't drive better results through fear and intimidation, which worked 100 years ago but not in today's labor market. At the other end of the spectrum, just being a nice person doesn't work, either. That may gain you friends in the short term, but it won't yield sustainably better operational outcomes.

The leadership mindset and everyday behaviors that make you a stronger, respected, more effective boss are much more nuanced. They require continuous self-reflection and an inherent personal improvement ethos that prioritizes people-centric leadership principles and practices over tactical achievement of discreet KPIs or financial targets.

In a word, bosses become great to work for because they are intentional and relentless in their efforts to show up better for their teams every day.

So, is all of this hard work really worth it? Research and personal experience show us that bad bosses survive all the time, often buried in organizational hierarchies that only hold them accountable for hitting operational and financial metrics in the short-term. The personal commitment to being a great boss has to go beyond KPIs.

Though few of us think about our long-term legacy when we're confronting immediate day-to-day issues, I've found that developing strong, mutually supportive relationships with employees at all levels can and should have enduring personal satisfaction. A few years ago, a college friend of my wife's shared a story that was both humbling and incredibly gratifying to me. Kristin, a physical therapist in Phoenix, discovered that one of her patients was a long-term employee at Phoenix Children's Hospital. She remarked, "A good friend's husband used to be the CEO at Phoenix Children's, but I'm sure you wouldn't know him because he left a long time ago. The patient asked, "Well, who is your friend?"

When Kristin told her that it was Burl Stamp, she smiled and said, "Oh, we remember Burl. He made a big impact because he really cared about employees."

Kristin shared that story with my wife eighteen years after I had left Phoenix Children's.

Lots of great memories came flooding back when my wife proudly told me that story. Yes, I did sincerely care about our dedicated staff and the special sacrifices they were making as we built the first freestanding children's hospital for Arizona families. But I also remember how much they cared about me and the sacrifices I was making at that time. Mutually beneficial relationships between a great boss and his or her hard-working team help everyone find more meaningful connection to purpose, realizing the impact that our work plays in achieving fulfillment in our personal lives.

ACKNOWLEDGMENTS

In many ways, this book belongs to the thousands of people who helped shape it. I am deeply grateful to those who worked alongside me, those who trusted me to lead them, and those who led and challenged me in return. Each relationship—whether as colleague, client, or mentor—taught me something meaningful about leadership, humility, and growth. The lessons I've learned from these individuals are woven throughout these pages.

I think I've gained the most wisdom from the strong leaders whom I've had the honor to work alongside as colleagues, especially the following individuals: Brian Smith, Velinda Block, Timm Glover, Nancy Litzinger, Patrick Lee, Kristi Roe, Pat Davis-Hagens, Bryan Mueller, Jason Niehaus, Patty Riskind, Rhonda Foster-Smith, Tom Peck, Sue Brandenberg, Ben Krueger, Sarah Hamilton Newell, and Steve Seiler.

My current Stamp & Chase colleagues, Alyssa Hwang and Ralph Wuebker, have been particularly helpful to me as I've contemplated important decisions related to our business, including writing this book.

I've had the good fortune of working for many strong bosses during my career who helped me recognize strengths I wanted to develop as well weaknesses I needed to remedy. Among them, I especially appreciate Joe Greskoviac, Nancy Loftin, Andy Bressler, Mike McGovern, Ed Pershing, and Nancy Mattson. Thank you for the significant wisdom you've shared that helped change the course of my career.

Outside of work, I've been blessed with a loving, supportive family, including our children (thank you Ben and Caroline for humoring Pops when he was often goofy), siblings, grandparents, aunts and uncles, and cousins. My mom has been most influential in helping me become the person I am today, always letting me chart my own path to success and learn from my own mistakes.

Most of all, I would never have made it this far in life without the support and encouragement of my wife Luanne. As my life partner, she's made me a much stronger person and leader. We make a damn good team that has hopefully modeled for our kids what a successful marriage looks like.

Finally, I'm humbly grateful for the skills God gave me. My hope is that I've been able to use some of those skills as a boss to help others find their own success, fulfillment, and happiness in life.

ABOUT THE AUTHOR

Since he was promoted to his first manager position at the age of twenty-two, Burl Stamp, FACHE, has been on a career-long journey to become a progressively better boss. For over twenty years as the president and founder of Stamp & Chase, he's helped thousands of other leaders in large and small organizations find their paths to being better bosses, as well.

Prior to launching Stamp & Chase, Burl served several leading health care organizations in executive roles, including President and CEO of Phoenix Children's Hospital and Vice President of Clinical Service Line Development for St. Louis Children's Hospital/BJC HealthCare.

He is the author of the book *The Healing Art of Communication,* a faculty member of the American College of Healthcare Executives, and has served on the Boards of Directors of Mercy Southeast, a regional health system serving southeast Missouri and southern Illinois, and the Society for Healthcare Strategy and Market Development of the American Hospital Association. His MBA degree is from Washington University in St. Louis, where he chaired the Olin Business School Alumni Association. He received his BSBA from Southeast Missouri State University.

Burl is a contemporary thought leader on emerging workforce challenges and a frequent speaker on communication, organizational culture, leadership effectiveness, and business development strategy. He and his wife Luanne live in the Central West End neighborhood of St. Louis and have two adult children, Ben and Caroline.

ENDNOTES

1   Gallup, Inc., State of the American Workplace (Washington, DC: Gallup, 2017), https://www.gallup.com/reports/199961/state-american-workplace-report-2017.aspx.

2   Rebecca Knight, "8 Essential Qualities of Successful Leaders," Harvard Business Review, December 8, 2023, https://hbr.org/2023/12/8-essential-qualities-of-successful-leaders.

3   "Monster Poll Finds One-Third of Employees Think Their Boss is 'Horrible,'" Recruiter.com, January 24, 2014, https://www.recruiter.com/recruiting/monster-poll-finds-one-third-of-employees-think-their-boss-is-horrible/.

4   "What Did the ACA Change About Health Coverage in the U.S.?" KFF, last modified October 8, 2025, https://www.kff.org/affordable-care-act/health-policy-101-the-affordable-care-act/?entry=table-of-contents-what-did-the-aca-change-about-health-coverage-in-the-u-s.

5   Courtney Davis et al., "Availability of Evidence of Benefits on Overall Survival and Quality of Life of Cancer Drugs Approved by European Medicines Agency: Retrospective Cohort Study of Drug Approvals 2009–13," The BMJ 359 (October 4, 2017): j4530, https://doi.org/10.1136/bmj.j4530.

6   Atul Gawande, The Checklist Manifesto: How to Get Things Right (New York: Metropolitan Books, 2009).

7   "Multitasking and How It Affects Your Brain Health," Brown University Health, accessed January 3, 2026, https://www.brownhealth.org/be-well/multitasking-and-how-it-affects-your-brain-health.

8   Herbert J. Freudenberger, "Staff Burn-Out," Journal of Social Issues 30, no. 1 (January 1974): 159–65, https://doi.org/10.1111/j.1540-4560.1974.tb00706.x.

9   Christina Maslach and Michael P. Leiter, The Truth About Burnout: How Organizations Cause Personal Stress and What to Do About It (San Francisco: Jossey-Bass, 1997).

10   Anjan V. Thakor and Robert E. Quinn, "When Work Has Meaning," Harvard Business Review, July–August 2018.

11   Kandi Wiens, "5 Characteristics of Stress-Resilient People (and How to Develop Them)," Harvard Business Review, February 2024.

12   Netta Weinstein, Andrew K. Przybylski, and Richard M. Ryan, "Paths to the Light and Dark Sides of Human Nature: A Meta-Analytic Review of the Prosocial Benefits of Autonomy and the Antisocial Costs of Control," Psychological Bulletin 147, no. 4 (2021): 343–382.

13   Paolo Gaudiano, "One More Time: Why Diversity Leads to Better Team Performance," Forbes, January 9, 2024.

14   Nishani Bourmault and Michael Anteby, "Research: Becoming a Manager Doesn't Always Feel Like a Step Up," Harvard Business Review, March 2024

15   David L. Cooperrider and Suresh Srivastva, "Appreciative Inquiry in Organizational Life," Research in Organizational Change and Development 1 (1987): 129–169.

16   Rebecca Knight, "Don't Let Lazy Managers Drive Away Your Top Performers," Harvard Business Review, March 2024.

17   Ethan Burris and James R. Detert, "Can Your Employees Really Speak Freely?" Harvard Business Review, January–February 2016.

18   George T. Doran, Arthur S. Miller, and James H. Cunningham, "There's a S.M.A.R.T. Way to Write Management's Goals and Objectives," Management Review 70, no. 11 (1981): 35–36.

19   Gallup, State of the American Manager: Analytics and Advice for Leaders (Washington, DC: Gallup, 2015).

20   Jack Zenger and Joseph Folkman, "The Ideal Praise-to-Criticism Ratio," Harvard Business Review, March 15, 2013, https://hbr.org/2013/03/the-ideal-praise-to-criticism.

21   Marcus Buckingham and Curt Coffman, First, Break All the Rules: What the World's Greatest Managers Do Differently (New York: Simon & Schuster, 1999)

22   Tracy Brower, "Empathy Is the Most Important Leadership Skill According to Research," Forbes, January 9, 2022.

23   Jean M. Twenge, Generations: The Real Differences between Gen Z, Millennials, Gen X, Boomers and Silents—and What They Mean for America's Future (New York: Atria Books, 2023).

Made in the USA
Monee, IL
07 July 2026

56546306R00132